# The Way I Went Last Friday

### HOW A TEENAGED SCHOOLGIRL REIGNED TERROR OVER THE CITY OF BUFFALO IN THE SUMMER OF 1961

Patrick Sawers

NFB Publishing
Buffalo, New York

NFB
NFB Publishing/Amelia Press
119 Dorchester Road
Buffalo, New York 14213

This book is dedicated to my partner in true crime,
Lauren B. Pelley

# Prologue

"I think I see a body in the water," the National Guardsman called out to his sergeant, who was standing maybe ten or fifteen feet back up along the bank.

Robert Kawczynski was a twenty-six-year-old lieutenant with the 127th Armor, First Medium Tank Battalion, stationed out of the Masten Avenue Armory on the city's east side.

It was day three of the search, and the forty-five men of his unit had been out there since daybreak, tracing the lake's perimeter for any sign of the missing child.

By now the entire city was on edge, alive with worry and talk of the brazen daytime kidnapping of a three-year-old boy, snatched right from his own front yard in a comfortable and orderly part of town. Law enforcement was working around the clock, with detectives doing house-to-house searches and police dogs sniffing every imaginable recess of the expansive park across from the victim's home. The fire department, local volunteer organizations and even civilian auxiliary units of the military were being called in to help search, and Kawczynski's battalion commander, Lieutenant Ronald Bolander, had offered up the use of his men accordingly.

The guardsmen had spread out along the northern shore of the eyebrow-shaped lake, scouring the surrounding land and carefully combing through the brush that lined the water's edge. Patrolling around the lake's easternmost end, shortly after two-thirty in the afternoon, Kawczynski caught sight of something in the water, something pale and unusual floating several feet from shore. Wading in shin-deep, the lieutenant soon recognized it as the lifeless body of a boy floating face-down and still, which he relayed to his nearest colleague, adding, "I don't want to disturb it. Get into the jeep and bring the police."

With that, Sergeant Stanley Rasprzak marked the spot with a length of timber and went motoring off, winding his way to the opposite end of the lake, where a police underwater recovery unit was stationed in a grand, three-story, Mediterranean-style casino. The team had been out there grappling since the previous day, and their captain, Charles DeVoe, was doing just that when Rasprzak arrived with the news. His men had already dragged the lake – twice, in fact – but access by boat to the parts nearest its shoreline was limited in general, and in this case it had been prohibited altogether by a slight patch of land that came jutting out into the water, forming a sort of harbor around the shallow area where Kawczynski had just made his discovery.

Captain DeVoe and five others - Detective Sergeant James Gibbons, Desk Lieutenant Rocco Navarro and patrolmen John Harris, Gerald Booker and Edward Conrad - quickly followed Rasprzak back to the scene, where it was sadly confirmed that the forty-two-hour citywide search had come to a heartbreaking close. There, roughly seven feet from shore and in about three feet of water, lie the deceased body of the missing boy.

With assistance from Navarro and Harris, Kawczynski carefully lifted the child's tiny corpse from the water, carrying it ashore and gently laying it out on the bank. And, right away, it was plain that the kid had met a harsh and terrifying demise. Dressed in nothing but a T-shirt and underwear, his hands and feet had been bound with women's nylon stockings and a dish towel secured tightly around his throat. The extent to which he had been interfered with while still alive was uncertain, but clearly the boy's abductor had been a cold-hearted fiend, murderous and deranged enough to whimsically extinguish the life of a helpless tot.

Reverend Daniel F. Kennedy, an ordained priest of the Oblate of Mary Immaculate and also an educator at nearby Bishop Fallon High School, had been summoned to the scene and he arrived short-ly. There, right on the jagged banks of the very lake which had just yielded the poor child's corporeal remains, the Reverend Kennedy administered the last rites of the Catholic church.

# ONE

## Something Wicked This Way Comes

It was the summer of 1961, and the city of Buffalo, New York, was still enjoying some of the postwar affluence that had largely defined the previous decade. Across the country young families were thriving, with employment readily available and wages that generally allowed for a home, a vehicle and a yearly vacation all on just one parent's salary. Their children, meanwhile, existed largely free-range, with evenings and weekends spent chiefly out of doors, out of sight and for the most part out of mind. Roaming the neighborhood was a youngster's birthright, and all was well so long as he or she made it home before the supper bell rang or the street lights came on.

Certainly this was the case in North Buffalo, where tree-lined streets bore comfortable homes and good neighbors, with little worry given to the thought of an unhinged psychopath prowling about with designs on all the kids. It was, in innumerable ways, a simpler place and time. The cornerstone of this area, then as now, was Delaware Park, a huge city park planted right in the midst of a bustling residential and business area, an instant escape into the rolling, pastoral countryside without having to even leave the city. At the northeastern tip of the park was the Buffalo Zoo, a long-time destination for families from across the region, where all summer long a steady flow of parents brought their kids to enjoy magical afternoons with the animals of the world.

Right across the street from the zoo, in the aptly-named Parkside neighborhood, a young couple occupied a small, basement apartment with their two children. Francis and Donna Ashley had come to Buffalo two years prior from Le Roy, a town not far from Rochester, about an hour to the east. Francis had graduated just two weeks earlier from Canisius College, a small, private Jesuit school a mile from their home, and he had just started a new job at an accounting firm in the Liberty Building downtown. Donna worked as a nurse at Buffalo General Hospital, and the couple had two kids – Andrew, a little over three, and Mark, not quite two.

At about four o'clock that Friday, June 23, Andrew had gone outside to play with a friend of his a few doors down. When he hadn't come back by six, Donna became concerned and walked over to check on him. There she found that no one was home, and that the friend's family was in fact out of town on vacation. With the shocking realization that her three-year-old boy had been missing and on his own for two full hours, Donna entered a maternal panic. She hastily assembled a small neighborhood search party, but by 9 p.m. police were on the scene and questioning everybody in the vicinity.

Soon detectives were speaking with a neighbor, Edwin Ehrne,

who claimed to have witnessed young Andrew, with whom he was familiar, being led away by a woman he had never seen before in his life. The kid had displayed a clear reluctance to go along with her, although at the time Ehrne had dismissed the strange lady as perhaps a visiting relative from out of town. The only real look he'd gotten at her was from behind, watching from his porch as she and Andrew walked hand in hand across the street toward the zoo entrance. His initial statement to police, it was reported the next day, was that the unfamiliar woman was "about the size of the boy's mother, who is 5 feet 5 inches and slim."

It wasn't much to go on. It had, however, established that the suspected abductor was a female – likely a surprise to most – and that she appeared to be early middle-aged. "A tall, slender woman in her mid-30s," ran one paper's description, while another depicted her as being "of medium build, about 35 years old, and having light hair." It was possible, one detective speculated, that the crazed kidnapper could be a woman "who may have suffered the loss of her own child through sickness or accidental injury."

Buffalo Police Commissioner Frank Felicetta, meanwhile, was overseeing the investigation personally, and all told he had around two hundred men out there working the case. They'd been tirelessly searching an area spanning roughly a mile and a half, with the fire department providing overhead lighting and canines tracking after the boy's scent, while back at the station detectives were fielding incoming tips from the general public. Even the FBI was involved, having opened up a child kidnapping case in accordance with the federally-enacted Lindbergh Law.

The local media, of course, were all over the story, bringing anxious city residents all the gripping details right as they unfolded.

Television was still a relatively-new medium, with nightly newscasts keeping viewers up to date with every breaking development in the case, a shocking and sensational true crime mystery set right in their own back yard. The city's two major newspapers, the *Buffalo Evening News* and the *Buffalo Courier-Express*, each were giving heavy coverage, with both publications appealing to readers for any information pertaining to the missing boy's whereabouts.

But now the story had pivoted. Breathless coverage of the search for three-year-old Andrew Ashley quickly gave way to sad reportage of the horrifying discovery of his drowned body. And, with that sickening jolt, so began one of the biggest manhunts in the city's history.

* * * * * *

Delaware Park Lake, the body of water from which workers had extracted the limp remains of Andrew Ashley, was not a lake at all, really. In truth it was an artificial widening of Scajaquada Creek, a thirteen-mile stream that starts in nearby Lancaster and twists and snakes its way west, passing through Buffalo just before emptying out into the Niagara River.

By the mid-nineteenth century the city of Buffalo was flourishing, rapidly becoming an industrial and manufacturing boomtown, well on its way to becoming one of the biggest cities in the country. In his 1866 report, city comptroller William Findlay Rogers pointed out the city's lack of a large public park space, something he considered essential for a bustling metropolis to thrive and maintain its expansion. Scajaquada Creek, he'd suggested, would provide a ready-made water source, one "from which artificial lakes could be supplied."

Two years later, upon being elected Buffalo's twenty-ninth mayor,

Rogers promptly went about laying the groundwork to create what would become Delaware Park, a 350-acre oasis woven right into the fabric of a still-sprawling urban environment. To design the space he'd hired the famed Olmsted, Vaux and Company, headed by Fredrick Law Olmsted, the country's premier landscape architect. His partner, Calvert Vaux, had been Olmsted's early mentor, and together the two had stunned the masses by unveiling New York's Central Park a decade earlier. Now, working in Buffalo from 1870 through 1874, the pair set out to accomplish something similar in majesty, if smaller in scale.

After securing a suitable tract of land – roughly the area between Forest Lawn Cemetery and what was then the Buffalo Normal School, now Buffalo State College – Olmstead and Vaux began laying the area out in two distinct and adjoining parts. Meadow Park, the eastern portion, would be a large, wide-open expanse populated with an abundance of trees, some walking paths and a sprinkling of wildlife (like wild sheep, grazing and lolling about the pasture). Water Park, to the west, was planned and designed around Scajaquada Creek, which was to be dammed off and opened up into a reservoir covering forty-plus acres of land.

Initially called Gala Water, the new "lake" featured prominently in the 1901 Pan-American Exposition, where it was viewed and admired by not one but two U.S. presidents (first by then-Vice President Theodore Roosevelt, on hand for the exposition's grand opening, and then by President William McKinley, soon to be felled by an assassin's bullet just a thousand or so feet from its northernmost shore). Over the next few decades it would come to be called Delaware Park Lake (or Park Lake, for short), and sites like the Albright-Knox Art Gallery and the Buffalo History Museum, each built right along its perimeter, helped make the spot a go-to destination for urban rec-reationalists, who turned out in droves to paddleboat there in the summer and to ice skate throughout the winter.

By 1961, though, the city of Buffalo, much like the country as a whole, was on the brink of considerable change. Mayor Frank A. Se-dita, a Democrat, was generally regarded as a firm and noble leader, stern but fair and eager to play his part in the ongoing reshaping of the city. Sedita, though, had a sweet tooth for the bulldozer, and he seemed to fully embrace the "urban renewal" trend that was then cropping up across the nation. He had recently overseen the dem-olition of his own childhood neighborhood, the Ellicott District, in an effort to redevelop the area into something better and more func-tional; within a decade the maneuver would be deemed a "dismal failure," having achieved little more than the displacement of about two thousand already-impoverished residents.

It was also under Sedita's leadership that a project was green-lit to link the city's east and west sides via a state highway, New York State Route 198. Also called the Scajaquada Expressway - so named because its path roughly retraces that of Scajaquada Creek - its first big stretch, beginning at Grant Street and extending as far east as Delaware Avenue, had just been laid and opened to traffic earlier in the year. Its remainder, built out over the following year, would go ripping right through the Delaware Park landscape, effectively bi-secting the park and creating two separate and distinct halves.

The lake, by this point, had been polluted and neglected for de-cades, and in recent years it had actually been closed to the public, declared a legitimate hazard by the Department of Health on ac-count of all the sewage that came flowing in via Scajacquada Creek. It had also been diminished considerably in size, with much of the surrounding land having since been filled in, as had just occurred at its northeastern end where the expressway's exit ramp (casually referred to as the "cloverleaf") passes within three hundred feet of where Andrew Ashley's body would be discovered.

These days, the lake is all cleaned up and back in business. Now called Hoyt Lake, renamed back in 1980 for Buffalo-born New York State Assemblyman Sam Hoyt, it's still a popular and lively warm-weather destination. Each summer city residents go there to relax around and about its shores, or to dine out on the patio of the Terrace at Delaware Park, a fancy-pants restaurant inside the Marcy Casino, where police had headquartered themselves while dragging the lake for the missing Ashley child.

And, just outside the casino, visitors today can rent pink flamingo-shaped paddleboats and make their way out onto the lake, perhaps venturing as far east as its opposite end near Delaware Avenue. There is now, at that point, a manmade fountain that sends a plume of water spraying fifty feet up into the air, an old underwater central jet spray system said to be left over from the Pan-Am Exposition days. Reinstalled between 2013 and 2017, the fountain is not just ornamental but also functional, doubling as an aerator that agitates and adds oxygen to the lake's typically-stagnant waters.

From that fountain, it is just a little over two hundred feet due north to the shoreline where Andrew Ashley's body was discovered. It is the closest thing there in the way of a monument to mark that mournful spot.

\* \* \* \* \* \*

"It was the summer Buffalo parents locked their children indoors," the *Buffalo Evening News* would later proclaim, revisiting and reflecting on the ordeal nearly thirty years after it transpired.

Almost overnight, it seemed, the city's youth were hustled inside and barred from leaving the house, or even their parents' sights, until the killer could be revealed, captured and locked away. The kidnapping and murder of Andrew Ashley was, in every way, a seismic event, one that bred a serious new anxiety into parents everywhere, and one that drastically redefined the landscape of youth culture by ushering in a whole new order of structure and supervision.

It is perhaps disconcerting, in hindsight, to read of children as young as three going outside to play by themselves in an urban environment, particularly in the context of that child then falling prey to some unconscionable predator. Still, in post-World War II America, that's essentially just the way it was. Back then kids played outside, alone and utterly unsupervised, often wandering off the block and sometimes getting lost. And yet, generally speaking, they could still be counted on to make it back on time and for the most part unscathed. Such was the norm because, in the summer of 1961, there simply was not much of a perceived threat.

This was something of a miscalculation, actually. In truth, this type of wickedness had breezed through the city of Buffalo on more than one occasion since the start of the twentieth century. Missing from the collective consciousness, at that time, was a looming awareness of two previous child homicides, each especially distressing and scandalous in their day, but both long-since faded from the headlines and largely forgotten to time.

Nearly six decades earlier, in the summer of 1902, an absolutely revolting crime occurred on the city's west side that bore some aching similarities to the Ashley case. Marian Murphy was five years old, and she lived with her parents near the corner of West Avenue and Pennsylvania Street. After dinner one evening she'd gone outside to play with a friend, and the two had gone off together to a nearby penny candy store. She'd allowed her friend a turn riding her bicycle, but when the girl refused to get off and give it back Marian got mad and stormed off. She never came back home.

A search was instituted, and right away the girl's disappearance was thought to be either a kidnapping or an accidental drowning in the nearby Erie Canal (it was just a ten-minute walk up Pennsylvania to where that street ended at the canal's filthy, polluted waters; this portion has since been filled in – the I-190 now passes directly over-head – but certainly back then these things did happen from time to time). It wasn't until ten days later that the girl was discovered dead, her body found by two employees patrolling a pond on the premises of Forest Lawn Cemetery. That pond lie right alongside Scajaquada Creek, less than a thousand yards from where it empties out into Delaware Park Lake, and just like poor Andrew the girl was found tied up and clad only in an undershirt. Unlike the Ashley kid, how-ever, Marian had been beaten and raped terribly, and she had not drowned but been strangled to death.

All suspicions, initially, were cast toward Marian's own father, Cornelius Murphy. Not only had the man acted pretty cagey in po-lice interviews, but his behavior around town both before and since his daughter's disappearance had sent up a lot of red flags. It was re-vealed that he suffered from paranoid, violent and explosive tenden-cies that had previously landed him in mental asylums, and stories were emerging that seemed to suggest even his own wife was fearful and distrusting of him.

Police surprised everyone, then, by instead arresting a man named

Charles We, one of a growing number of Chinese immigrants then settling in and around the neighborhood. We, the proprietor of a "Chinese laundry" just around the corner on Hudson Street, was arrested following a search of his premises that had turned up a few items of interest, including a pair of loaded revolvers and some fabric similar to the material used in the disposal of Marian's body. As evidence it was flimsy and circumstantial at best, and when the grand jury refused to indict prosecutors were left understandably unenthused about then trying the girl's father for the exact same crime. The murder of Marian Murphy was never solved.

Less than a decade later, in the fall of 1911, another child went missing, this time just several miles south of the city in nearby Lackawanna, then a young and bustling steel and manufacturing town. Seven-year-old Joey Joseph lived with his family on Ridge Road, Lackawanna's main drag, where his father George also owned and operated a clothing shop. The Josephs were hardworking and ambitious Syrian immigrants, well-known and well-regarded in their community. One October evening, while playing outside in front of his home, Joey and a friend were approached by an older gentleman who offered to take them to the candy store across the street. The friend later told police that, after sending Joey inside with a few pennies, the man then directed him to run along home on his own. It was the last time anyone would see the Joseph kid alive.

Within weeks, some unknown person began engaging police and the boy's parents in a cruel course of one-way correspondence, a string of letters and postcards in which he bragged to have killed the child in the moments immediately following his disappearance. These communications, thought to be a hoax at first, continued for a full year, and in them the grim circumstances of the kid's death would be revealed: from the candy shop the man had led his victim next door to an outhouse behind Doyle's Saloon (at 121 Ridge Road, a Family Dollar is there today), where he choked and raped the boy before strangling him to death and stuffing his body down into the rancid pit beneath. It was not until the following November that Joey Joseph's badly-decomposed remains were finally located and fished out of precisely that spot.

And when the *Buffalo Evening News* then ran facsimiles of those chilling postcards on its front page, the handwriting was soon recognized as belonging to 46-year-old John Frank Hickey, a foreman at the Lackawanna Steel Company (later to become widely known as Bethlehem Steel). Hickey, it turned out, was a lifelong drifter, a ne'er-do-well and a bad alcoholic whose struggles with "demon whiskey," as he put it, fueled an unmanageable drive to abuse children and extinguish life. It was soon learned that he had also been the murderer of eleven-year-old Michael Kruck, a newsboy found strangled to death in New York's Central Park back in 1902, and that he'd poisoned a coworker nearly three decades earlier in his hometown of Lowell, Massachusetts. Hickey was located and arrested within a week, then tried, convicted and sentenced to life at Auburn State Prison.

All of that was long forgotten by the summer of 1961, however, as Buffalo residents found themselves stunned and feeling absolutely blindsided by the taking and drowning of one of their own, an innocent young life snuffed out at random and for no real reason at all. It was odd, of course, that the perpetrator thought to be responsible for such a horrendous thing should be a female; traditionally, senseless acts of violence and murder have been the domain of maladjusted or otherwise unstable men. Still, as an entire city now awaited the killer's capture, it did so with the expectation that authorities eventually would arrest and present some sort of crazed, middle-aged madwoman.

It was another cold shock, then, when that day came and the culprit finally was unmasked. It was the single most-anticipated capture and arrest in recent memory, with the general public half-expecting a menacing and depraved adult woman, possibly with horns and fangs and all of that business. The big, bad wolf of North Buffalo, however, had merely been masquerading in the garment of an older woman.

Instead, and to the complete astonishment of an entire city, the villain they had all dreaded turned out to be something of a child herself, a sweet-looking fifteen-year-old schoolgirl named Chyrel Jolls.

\* \* \* \* \* \*

A quick note regarding the curious spelling of this girl's first name. Chyrel, generally pronounced "Shirelle," is French in origin with a meaning of "darling, beloved." According to the website names.org, the Social Security Administration between 1880 and 2020 recorded a total of only 265 children being assigned that unusual name at birth, the first-known instance occurring in 1888. In 1945, the year prior to Chyrel's birth, just seven babies had that name entered onto their birth certificates. Its highest-known usage came over a decade later, in 1957, with twenty such instances recorded.

In their reportage of the coming events, the city's two major newspapers were divided on the proper spelling of their subject's first name. Although the *Buffalo Courier-Express* would spell it correctly, its rival, the *Buffalo Evening News*, would consistently, and incorrectly, print her name as "Cheryl." While this book utilizes the correct spelling – confirmed via court records obtained from the Erie County Court's criminal records department – when quoting directly from the latter publication the misspelling of "Cheryl" has been preserved.

# TWO

## An Ungovernable Minor

FIFTEEN-YEAR-OLD CHYREL L. Jolls was not native to the Buffalo area, and she hadn't grown up like most kids her age.

Born January 4, 1946, she had spent her earliest years in Westfield, a small town about sixty miles west of the city, just a stone's throw from the Pennsylvania line. The fourth of seven children born to Howard and Georgia Jolls, Chyrel's childhood had consisted largely of familial turmoil and financial instability. Howard, an electrician by trade, seems to have struggled with alcoholism and unemployment throughout much of his adult life, leaving to his wife the unenviable task of raising and managing their considerable brood.

Poverty and domestic chaos had haunted the family from the very start, with periodic relocations across Western New York and their various children constantly in and out of foster homes. Beginning in the 1950s the family started inching their way west, living briefly in the tiny town of Ellington before moving to nearby Dayton and, later, South Dayton.

Chyrel's siblings, meanwhile, one by one were falling out of the picture, with three of them – Estelle, Clara and Barbara – ending up in foster care and the eldest two – Alvin and Henry – reaching adulthood and wisely set out on their own. By the close of the decade only two of Howard and Georgia's kids – Chyrel and her youngest sister Nora – remained legally in their care.

Chyrel, for her part, had always been an especially problematic child. She too had been placed in a series of foster homes over the years, where her defiant and troublesome behavior had consistently proven too much for her caretakers. She later admitted, for instance, to setting several small fires in a few of these residences, and twice she'd had to spend a bit of time in mental institutions. The first of these was the Newark State School, an asylum in the Central New York village of Newark, and following another incident she'd been sent for observation at Rochester's Strong Memorial Hospital.

It has since been reported that, in at least one of these facilities, Chyrel was subjected to a variety of medical treatment that was then in vogue but soon to come under considerable social scrutiny. Electroconvulsive therapy, or ECT, had become commonplace in hospitals by the 1950s, and it worked by inducing mild and controlled seizures via an electrical current. "There is no question that ECT was benefitting patients then," wrote Jonathan Sadowsky, a historian of psychiatry, in a 2017 essay for an online publication called *the Conversation*, "but there is also a lot of evidence from that period showing that ECT, and the threat of it, were used in mental hospitals to control difficult patients and to maintain order on wards."

Upon her release from Strong Memorial it was initially uncertain where Chyrel, then twelve, would live. Given her parents' glaring inability to function as such, an aunt volunteered to lighten their load by taking Chyrel in with her. Estelle Ott, Georgia's sister, lived just across the Canadian border in Welland, Ontario, with seven kids of her own. And while she graciously offered her niece a place under her roof, Canadian immigration authorities nixed that plan on the grounds that Estelle had enough on her plate without some trouble-making American relation swelling her burden.

By late 1958 Howard had landed in some trouble again (presumably alcohol was involved), and he had been remanded to the facilities at Gowanda State Hospital, now a part of Gowanda Correctional Facility. Chyrel, at the time, was spending weekends with her aunt up in Welland, and Estelle would later remark that her father's ongoing incarceration seemed only to exacerbate the girl's already disquieting behavior. Once, she said, when Chyrel was told that no mail for her had arrived from Gowanda, she'd broken down and become physically violent.

There was another, more disturbing incident to follow. After taking one of her aunt's young sons out for a walk one day, Chyrel returned saying she'd lost track of the boy somewhere along the way. Estelle remained in a maternal tizzy until later that day, when the kid was located in a tiny room at the back of the house, bound hand and foot and no doubt scared out of his little mind. Chyrel swore up and down she'd had nothing to do with it, but her aunt knew better and communicated to Georgia that they seemed to have a profoundly disturbed young girl on their hands.

\* \* \* \* \* \*

SURE enough, Chyrel soon was off for another spell in supervised living, this time at the Good Shepherd Home, a local detention facility for "ungovernable minors."

Run by the Sisters of the Good Shepherd, a Roman Catholic order for pious women, the convent's stated goal was to shelter and reform "fallen and abandoned" young girls. That phrase, it's worth noting, in the parlance of the mid-twentieth century often translated roughly into "unwed and with child." And while there has never been any overt mention of Chyrel having gotten pregnant (she would have been just twelve at the time), certainly such matters were not discussed freely in those days and, given the facility's utter lack of transparency, it is not entirely outside the scope of possibility.

Listed at 485 Best Street, the compound occupied nearly an entire city block on the city's impoverished east side, sitting slightly-elevated atop a meager hill and walled off by a twelve-foot-high stone barricade. Inside, the place was very much the disciplined fortress its stern exterior suggested, run much like a prison, only perhaps more so. It was, in fact, what was known as a "Magdalene asylum," or a "Magdalene laundry," one of a handful across the country run by the Good Shepard sisters. Functioning as a sort of community laundry drop-off for the surrounding neighborhood, residents earned their keep by toiling daily in the unimaginable heat of what amounted to nothing short of an underground sweatshop.

And while the facility would be shuttered by the mid-to-late 1960s, a lawsuit filed in late 2019 alleges publicly what's long been whispered in private. According to its plaintiff (whose tenure there predated Chyrel's by about two years), upon admission she was ushered into a room and visited by an (alleged) physician who, under the guise of performing an "internal medical examination," proceeded to interfere with her sexually. The suit, allowed for under New York's 2019 Child Victim Act, implies that this procedure was routine and widespread.

Perhaps predictably, Chyrel did not thrive there. On January 21, 1959, a small fire broke out on the grounds, yielding around $200 damage. Chyrel and another girl, also twelve, were questioned at length by police investigators, and eventually the other girl fingered Chyrel as the guilty party. When pressed by Sergeant Fred Thomasula of the arson squad, Chyrel explained that she'd started the blaze in hopes of getting transferred to Gowanda, where at least she would be near her father. In his report, Thomasula described her as "very defiant" and "very antagonistic."

A typical stay at the Good Shepherd Home generally spanned twelve months, so Chyrel's season there would have concluded by the end of that year. The convent would itself close down by the end of the decade, although the property today is largely unchanged and still very much mired in secrecy. In the aftermath of 9/11, for instance, concerns were raised publicly that its present owners, a sort of Islamic cultural center called Darul-Uloom Al-Madania, were utilizing its underground tunnels and such as a training cell for future terror attacks.

From the outside, though, its grounds remain ominous and foreboding and essentially as they were back then – largely untouched and aesthetically frozen in time.

\* \* \* \* \* \*

WITH her husband still away at Gowanda, Georgia Jolls had been struggling considerably as a single mother. Luckily she had another sibling, a brother in Buffalo, and he'd offered to help out by taking Chyrel in while Georgia hunted for suitable quarters somewhere in the city.

John Palmer lived with his wife Eugenia in North Buffalo, and he was employed as a tool cutter at the Chevrolet Motors plant on East Delevan Avenue. Apparently he went by Jack, while his wife went by Jean. The *Buffalo Courier-Express* would later describe the couple's "neat, second-story apartment" at 510 Tacoma Avenue, a nice-sized two-story house in the North Park neighborhood. There, it seems, Chyrel was welcomed into a warm and caring home environment, with a pair of stable adults who seemed actively engaged and genuinely glad to have her there. She would end up staying for five months.

"She enjoyed doing the simplest things," Palmer would later tell the *Buffalo Evening News*, "like going downtown on Saturday night to window-shop. She had never seen the Falls, so we took her there. And she was thrilled over a $1.40 trip to see Niagara Falls." In time she grew friendly with some of the local kids, and Chyrel often would take the couple's year-old dog out for long strolls around the neighborhood.

At the same time, Palmer said, his niece hardly seemed to be entirely at ease. "If we went into a restaurant for a soft drink, she would wring her hands and tear a paper napkin to bits," he told the *Evening News*. "She would ask me, 'Do you really love me, Uncle Jack?'" To the *Courier-Express*, he remarked: "She sometimes would wring her hands violently while she was talking; her problems were too deep for me." He and Chyrel regularly attended Sunday services at Calvary Gospel Tabernacle (at 1722 Main Street, the church is still in operation, now called the Midtown Bible Church), and Palmer did note that it seemed to be a rare source of comfort. "When she was particularly upset," he said, "I sometimes would read to her from the Bible, and that would make her feel better."

It wasn't long, however, before he'd started calling around, seeing what type professional help might be available for his high-strung and anxiety-ridden young niece. He'd "asked in lots of places for help," Palmer explained to the *Courier-Express*, "but everyone seems to pass the buck to someone else; they just want to wash their hands of it." To the *Evening News* he remarked: "They would say: 'We will call you back.' But they never did." Ultimately, he concluded, there were no systems in place and no one who really cared enough to wind through all the bureaucratic red tape.

Eventually Georgia did manage to find a place in Buffalo, so Chyrel soon rejoined her mother and her sister Nora, as well as all the stressful uncertainty that generally clings to broken and impoverished families. Conditions there were in stark contrast to those she'd known while staying with the Palmers, but she visited her uncle and aunt often and wound up spending alternating weekends with them. It was, her uncle later stated flatly, "her second home."

The apartment her mother had secured was a couple miles south of there, closer to downtown and on the outskirts of the Parkside neighborhood. It occupied the second floor of 21 Leroy Avenue, a gray house with green shingles just a few doors down from that street's intersection with Main (the house has since been demolished, and the tiny lot remains vacant to this day). Georgia had managed to find work in the cafeteria at nearby Buffalo General Hospital, and she'd begun regularly attending Prospect Avenue Baptist Church on the city's west side.

Just steps away from their new home – right across the intersection diagonally – stood Buffalo Public School 54, where Chyrel, now fourteen, was enrolled into the seventh grade. This placed her about three years behind her peers, that considerable gap likely owing as much to her rocky upbringing as it did to the mental difficulties with which she'd always struggled. These factors alone would have made her something of an outcast, and she was likely isolated further by the fact that she stood out physically as well: at around five-foot-five, she stood a good three inches taller than most girls her age, giving her the appearance of being decidedly older than she really was.

The seas were still pretty choppy at home, too. Although it was just the three of them there, they were apparently struggling at times just to keep food on the table. A 1990 article in the *Buffalo Evening News* claimed that neighbors at the time had reported repeated "requests to borrow a few potatoes for dinner," as well a bunch of "shouting that came from their house" in general. They also spoke of "the night the School 54 student was seen standing on a crate, a pop bottle in her hand, swaying and singing to a full moon."

She spent as much time as possible at her "second home," visiting her Uncle Jack and her Aunt Jean at their apartment roughly every other weekend. Around this time, her uncle later told the *Courier-Express*, boys started coming around to take her out on what he called "milkshake dates."

In fact, by February 1961, there was one boy in particular. At a local skating rink she'd met a 16-year-old from Hertel Avenue (his name was withheld from the press), and he would later tell authorities that since that time they had gone on approximately fifteen dates. These, he explained, were casual afternoon affairs, usually involving a trip to a downtown movie theater or a leisurely stroll through Delaware Park. One time, the boy recalled, they'd planned a picnic in the park and Nora had tagged along, but soon the sisters were at each other's throats and Chyrel chased Nora off.

A few final glimpses into Chyrel's life in the spring of 1961 were to be found in her own writings, a few sheets of loose-leaf notebook paper which would in the coming weeks be seized by police. They seemed to constitute a makeshift diary, and heading the pages was the declaration, "This is my own account of how I think and do things – also why I do them." The first entry was from March 22, and it referenced an alarming interaction with a man who gave her some "white pills." She made no mention of their effects or what they might have been, but certainly it's interesting to know that an already-unsettled teen may have been out there operating under the influence of some unidentified narcotic. On April 10, she wrote, she'd taken her aunt and uncle's dog out for a walk and lost it.

That April Howard was paroled from Gowanda. He'd rejoined his wife and two daughters at 21 Leroy, where he struggled with finding work and also with staying sober. The *Courier-Express* would describe him as "a middle-aged man of small build with greying hair," while the *Evening News* noted that he was "a thin man, not quite short." Neither paper seems to have found him especially remarkable, painting instead the picture of a meek and timid man – uninvolved, defeated by the bottle and hardly fit to be the head of a family. But Georgia had her job at the hospital cafeteria, and with that income the family hobbled on and continued scraping by.

# THREE

## Susie

At the southwest corner of Commonwealth and Tacoma Avenues, about a mile above the northernmost tip of Delaware Park, stands a condominium-style brick apartment building that looks to be well over a century old. Listed at 299 Tacoma, the place was, in 1961, then named the Calumet Apartments, where unit fourteen was home to John and Judith Benedict, as well as their five-year-old daughter Susan.

April 23 was a Sunday, and Chyrel had spent that weekend with the Palmers, whose place was also on Tacoma, just five blocks up the road. At around 5 p.m. she set out walking, and as she passed the Calumet she spotted Susan, playing alone out in its open courtyard. Chyrel had, as her uncle would later point out, a tendency to stop and engage with younger kids, and kids seemed to respond well to her friendly chatter and deceptively childlike demeanor.

Susan Benedict was no exception. In a 2012 article published in the online journal *Truro News*, Canadian true crime writer Max Haines revisited their interaction that day, indicating that Susan had been out there playing hopscotch when Chyrel made her approach. "As she stood on one foot maintaining her balance," wrote Haines, "Susie was approached by a young friendly lady, who asked her if she would like to take a walk. It was such a nice day and the lady was so friendly, Susie went along willingly."

It's doubtful Susan had pictured herself being gone too long or straying very far; they were headed north on Commonwealth, which reaches its terminus just one block up at Taunton Place. As they walked, Susan later told police, she noticed Chyrel was eating candy – Tootsie Rolls and Jawbreakers, specifically – a trifling detail which would nonetheless become significant in the coming months. At the street's end stood perpendicularly a line of homes, and beyond those were some railroad tracks. Chyrel managed to coax the girl back there and off into some brush, pausing at what Haines called "a weed-infested field near a little-used railroad siding."

Then, in a flash, everything about Chyrel seemed to change. "Suddenly," wrote Haines, "the lady became angry and threw the child to the ground." Susan started sobbing, and "as she did so, the angry lady removed the terrified child's shoes and socks. The socks were stuffed into Susie's mouth to stifle her crying while her laces were removed and used to tie her hands and feet." The *Buffalo Evening News*, for its part, noted that Susan's own "jacket belting" also was involved in tying her up. Both agree on what happened next: Chyrel, apparently satisfied with whatever it was she'd just accomplished, simply walked away.

"Susie struggled to free her hands and feet," Haines wrote, "but found the task impossible." Eventually she managed to spit out her socks, and the girl's subsequent cries for help attracted the attention of an older kid who came and untied her. "A teenaged boy heard her screams, scrambled down the embankment and untied the laces around her hands and feet," wrote Haines. "He escorted her to a nearby house. It was only a matter of minutes before the girl's parents and police were notified."

Susan was questioned at length by police, and according to Haines "an extensive search for her abductor was immediately instituted." The description she was able to provide them with was tenuous at best – essentially that her kidnapper had appeared to be roughly "as old as mommy, but not as old as grandma." As they'd walked, she recalled, the woman mentioned she lived nearby in a big, blue house with her mother and six children; its address, she had claimed, was 2290, but provided no street name.

Two weeks later, while riding in the car with her mother, Susan spotted someone who resembled Chyrel walking into a Fillmore Avenue store, pointing her out as "the woman who tied me up." Perhaps it was, and perhaps it wasn't. But with so little to go on, Haines noted, there was only so much police investigators could really do, and "slowly the abduction took a back seat to more pressing matters."

# FOUR

## Ritchie

Two months passed without incident, at least so far as anyone knows. In June she'd graduated the seventh grade at School 54, and with classes out for the summer Chyrel was largely free to roam the city. And, as always, she remained a regular fixture at her aunt and uncle's place up on Tacoma Avenue.

Given the amount of time she was spending with the Palmers and in their neighborhood, it's natural that Chyrel would gravitate toward its epicenter, Hertel Avenue. Much like it is today, Hertel was then a friendly and community-oriented strip of commercial and residential interests, its vibrant cultural demographic taking shape as longtime Jewish denizens were blending with a recent influx of Italians migrating from the city's west side. The strip's main hotspot, back then, was the North Park Theatre (at 1428 Hertel), where neighborhood kids like herself could spend entire Saturdays eating pop-corn and watching endless matinees, if they weren't passing the time drinking sodas or milkshakes in a nearby drug store.

Just a block west of the theater, at the northeast corner of Her-tel's intersection with Saranac Avenue, there stands a property that's pretty typical of this part of the Hertel strip - a long, two-level brick building with residences up top and a few businesses side by side at street level (in 1961 these included the Variety Dress Shop at 1374, and also the Stocking Bar at 1370). The building rounds the corner onto Saranac, where the upstairs space – marked 81 Saranac – was home to John Edgington, a worker at the nearby Linde Air Products Factory, as well as his wife Judith and their young son Richard.

Richard Edgington – or Ritchie, as he was called back then – was just five years old, and on the afternoon of Thursday, June 22, he was outside playing hide and seek with a bunch of the neighbor-hood kids. Photos of him from this time show what appears to be an imaginative and precocious young explorer, and atop his buzz-cut head that afternoon he wore a kid-sized pith helmet (also known as a sun helmet, it's a safari-style hat made of lightweight metal and covered in cloth, designed to keep the brush out of your face and the sunshine out of your eyes). His mother Judith would later testify that he'd left their residence at around 1:35 p.m.

It was a little over an hour later that Chyrel came strolling along, arriving at Hertel and Saranac just in time to find Ritchie standing right outside his home. Chyrel, for her part, was dressed neatly and presentably; police would later provide the papers with the specifics of her attire: a "one-piece, grayish-blue dress with perpendicular blu-ish-gray stripes and small flowered design, also running perpendic-ularly," along with "what appeared to be new high-heeled shoes and hose," her hair done up in "a short pony tail through a metal ring."

Her approach, Ritchie would later tell the author Catherine Pelonero, was an unimaginative variation of the classic kid-snatcher come-on: "My mother is with your mother and you're supposed to come with me." Instinctively his young mind knew to doubt this, and perhaps sensing the kid's skepticism Chyrel tried to sweeten the pot by offering to take him to the zoo. Eventually, though, she grew impatient and cut right to the chase, declaring, "If you don't come with me, I'll drown you." In his petrified confusion Ritchie agreed to do as she said, and a witness, viewing the interaction from her workplace across the street, would later testify to seeing Chyrel lead the boy away, taking him by the hand and heading north up Saranac.

A block up the pair came to Tacoma, where they turned right and continued on for four or five more blocks. As they did, Ritchie later told police, Chyrel starting eating candy – Tootsie Rolls in particular – and she hadn't been too keen on sharing, promising instead to give him one *eventually*, so long as he didn't run away or start to cry. Soon Chyrel decided to cut back over toward Hertel, so they hung right on what police later surmised was likely Frontenac Avenue, the one side street in the area that doesn't quite make that connection (it's cut off by Lyndhurst Avenue, requiring a quick jog around two additional corners to get there).

Because of this Chyrel became confused, and when she spotted a man sitting out on his front porch she approached to ask directions to Hertel. Ritchie would describe this house to investigators "as having either a white fence or a white porch railing," the *Buffalo Courier-Express* reported, and the man in question apparently got them back on track, as Ritchie recalled reaching Hertel and Parkside Avenue a short while later. Following that interaction, though, the boy said Chyrel had issued a further directive: "She told me if anybody stopped and talked with me I was to tell the person my name was Davie Johnson."

They proceeded south on Parkside. Chyrel, it seems, had meant what she'd said about taking Ritchie to the zoo, which lay another six blocks ahead, right on the northeastern edge of Delaware Park. They'd wound up walking on the left-hand side of the road, and just past Linden Avenue, where a stone railroad viaduct crosses over Parkside, Chyrel again fell into conversation with some passersby. This time it was a young couple, possibly folks she was acquainted with, and she likely wasn't prepared to explain Ritchie's presence. There were, at that time, freestanding, antique-style light posts lining the sidewalk every fifty feet or so, so Chyrel had him run ahead and hide behind one of them while they stopped to chat a bit. Ritchie couldn't really hear their conversation, he told investigators, but the exchange seemed to last "several minutes."

Two blocks ahead, at Parkside's intersection with Amherst Avenue, lie the main entrance court to what was then the crown jewel of the North Buffalo experience. Established in 1875, the Buffalo Zoo was one of the oldest in the country, and it had been built out considerably by President Franklin D. Roosevelt's Works Progress Administration. Admission at the time was still free, and after crossing back over Parkside Chyrel and Ritchie bypassed the zoo's main gate, traveling instead a block up Amherst and utilizing a secondary entrance at Colvin Avenue.

Upon entering, Ritchie later recalled, the first exhibit he and Chyrel encountered was Monkey Island. A bland-looking garage-type building stands there today, but Monkey Island back then was home to dozens of wily primates frolicking freely on a big, man-made, moated-off rockpile replete with a swimming pool and trapeze system. Bypassing the huge, horseshoe-shaped building that housed the lions, tigers and other mammals, Chyrel and Ritchie made their way toward the zoo's center, where the boy paused to take notice of the Seal Pool (another WPA project, also since torn down and hauled away) before moving on to view a collection of caged eagles.

Ritchie, by this point, was getting tired and beginning to complain, so he and Chyrel paused for a rest at nearby gate eight, where the kid did his best to draw from a public water fountain, struggling a bit with its foot-operated pedal. It was here, Ritchie later told police, that Chyrel finally relented and let him have a piece of the candy she'd been consuming the whole time. "She ate a lot of candy, especially Tootsie Rolls," he explained, "but I got one piece. She kept on eating and wouldn't give me any more."

With that they quit the zoo, stepping out into the portion of Delaware Park known as the Meadow, a wide-open patch of land featuring, amongst other things, a large and well-maintained cricket field. Toward the center of that field, marking the burial spot of three hundred men killed in the war of 1812, two huge cannons from that era were stationed alongside a flagpole and a large rock. Here, Ritchie recalled, he and Chyrel rested a bit more before picking up and walking on (the cannons and the flagpole have since been removed, but that boulder remains in place, resting between two weeping willows near the second hole of what is now the park's golf course).

From there they trotted carelessly right out onto the open cricket greens, swiftly attracting the attention of a nearby groundskeeper named Sam Costa, who called out to them from atop his gasoline-powered lawnmower. "He was sitting on a loud grasscutter," Ritchie would later recall. "I couldn't hear what he was saying because the grasscutter was loud, but I knew he was mad at the lady for being on the grass." Costa himself would later confirm this, telling investigators he had chased a lady off the greens for wearing high heels.

Perhaps spooked by Costa's gruff reproach, Chyrel decided to leave the park altogether, taking Ritchie and exiting alongside the zoo, roughly where they'd come in. They started back toward Hertel, but just two blocks north they encountered the New York Central Railroad tracks running perpendicularly, part of what was called the Belt Line Railroad. Together they made their way up its embankment and started following the tracks east, and when Ritchie started whimpering Chyrel punched him in the arm repeatedly. Gesturing to a nearby puddle of water, the boy would later recall, she glared at him and threatened, "This is where I'm going to drown you and you'll never see your mother or father again."

Several minutes later they reached the overpass near Parkside and Linden, right above the spot where Chyrel had stopped to chat with an unknown couple before reaching the zoo. Now elevated and out of sight from the traffic below, Chyrel announced that the time had come for she and Ritchie to play Cowboys and Indians. Taking the helmet from his head and placing it on her own, Chyrel then removed Ritchie's clothes – his shirt, his pants, his shoes – and tied his hands and feet with some twine she'd gathered along the way. Next, police later told the *Buffalo Evening News*, "she took a jaw-breaker from her mouth and put it into the Edgington boy's mouth before gagging him." After pulling a plastic bag down over his head, Chyrel – abruptly and without explanation – concluded she had done enough and was through for the day.

Leaving the kid right there to struggle helplessly, she continued alone along the railroad tracks, which wrap around to the south and, if followed long enough, actually cross under Leroy Avenue less than a block from her home. She still had Ritchie's clothes and his pith helmet with her, and as she walked – about a quarter-mile along, according to the *Evening News* – she carelessly discarded these items by tossing them off into some bushes.

Ritchie, for his part, got lucky: he was a tough kid who quickly managed to free himself, waiting until his abductor was gone and then kicking his feet loose and working the bag off his head. Rather than double back he scrambled along the tracks a bit further, and in order to get back to the street he had to make his way up a steep hill and over a fence.

"I broke the ropes on my feet and I climbed up the embankment with my hands tied behind my back," he would tell investigators. "I was able to get the gag out of my mouth and ripped the plastic bag with my teeth." Emerging into someone's backyard on Linden Avenue, Ritchie climbed over a chicken wire fence and made his way out into the street. "And that's where a woman saw me and she took me into her house and called the police."

It was about 4 p.m. when Ritchie was spotted and ushered inside the home of Mr. and Mrs. James Phillips, a two-story house at 33 Linden Avenue. Finding the young kid dirtied, bruised about the face and with his hands still tied behind his back, Mrs. Phillips immediately telephoned the boy's mother, who came rushing over to gather her son at once.

All told Ritchie had been in Chyrel's clutches for two and a half hours, and no one had even known he was missing or in any sort of danger. But after seeing his marked-up face, and upon hearing him tell of how he'd come to turn up a mile from home and all out of sorts, John and Judith Edgington decided to contact police.

The next day John made a formal report, filing a third-degree assault complaint against an unknown party, identified in their paperwork only as "Mary Doe." Investigators, though, would not have so much as an afternoon to follow up in earnest.

# FIVE

## Andy

The brief kidnapping of Richard Edgington, actually, appears to have been something of a trial run. Within twenty-four hours Chyrel was right back out and about, apparently determined to pick up more or less where she'd left off.

Friday, June 23, was a bit cooler than usual, with rain falling intermittently all throughout the afternoon. By around 4 p.m. Chyrel was back in the Delaware Park area, prowling along Parkside Avenue just outside the zoo's eastern perimeter. Just across the street, where Jewett Parkway reaches its terminus at Parkside, she came to a three-story, condo-style brick apartment building on the northeast corner.

195 Jewett Parkway, today, is part of the Parkview Garden Apartments, which include another building that extends north on Parkside. At that time, though, basement apartment A was home to

the Ashley family, who had moved to Buffalo three years earlier from the town of Le Roy, thirty miles outside of Rochester. Twenty-six-year-old Francis C. Ashley had recently claimed an accounting degree from Canisius College, and his wife Donna, also twenty-six, was a registered nurse at nearby Buffalo General Hospital. The couple had two children. Their youngest, Mark, was not quite two years old, and as such he gobbled up much of his parents' time and attention. Andrew, the couple's oldest, was a little over three and, perhaps by necessity, remarkably independent for his young age.

Andrew T. Ashley was born in February 1958, and nearly his entire life had been spent in and around that residence. Neighbors knew him as a sweet, bright and precocious little kid – "an intelligent boy in the opinion of neighbors," as the *Buffalo Courier-Express* would later put it. With short blonde hair and bright blue eyes, his photographs show what can only be a cheerful, bubbly and sometimes impish young tot. He was, his mother insisted, "a real friendly boy, but sometime shy with strangers."

Just before 4 p.m. Andy asked his mother for permission to go outside and play with some of the other kids on the block. Specifically, he told her, he wanted to go see his friend Ronald Laux, who lived right around the corner and had a sandbox in his yard. The Laux family resided just a few houses up, at 251 Parkside, and their backyard could be accessed by cutting through those of a few easygoing and indifferent neighbors. Donna knew Andy and Ronald liked to spend hours at a time in that sandbox, so without much hesitation she allowed her boy to head out and over there on his own.

One house beyond the Laux place, at 255 Parkside, Edwin J. Ehrne was sitting out on his front porch, where he'd been for about an hour. Ehrne, who had nine grandchildren of his own, knew and was friendly with the Ashley boy, later telling the *Buffalo Evening News* that "the kid was in here four or five times a day," and that he would give him "suckers or a nickel or dime" to run along with. Now, looking up he spotted Andy - dressed in a brown T-shirt, olive checkered pants and blue sneakers - at just about the moment he was being approached by a woman Ehrne did not recognize.

He watched as the lady took Andy by the hand and led him directly across Parkside, and to Ehrne it seemed as if the kid had been reluctant to accompany her. "I thought nothing of it at the time," he would tell the *Evening News*, "because I thought it was an aunt or some relative taking him to see the animals." The zoo was directly across the street, and it had an entrance another half-block up, where Russell Street ends at Parkside. Ehrne reported watching them enter the zoo at that point, utterly clueless to the fact that it would mark the last time anyone would see the boy alive.

According to his autopsy, Andy Ashley drew his last breath somewhere around 5 p.m., roughly an hour after his brazen abduction. No one knows, and no one ever will know, the exact specifics of what transpired during that time. Apparently they visited the zoo, and after that it's believed they continued out into the park, just as Chyrel had done a day earlier and with a different child.

Meadow Drive, the two-lane road that wraps around this part of the park, has for many years been closed to vehicular traffic. At that time, however, motorists were still permitted to cruise the Meadow's nearly-two-mile perimeter, and the occupants of one car in particular would later report seeing something unusual just as they passed its westernmost tip, the Point of the Meadow. A yellow-brick shelter house stood there, as it still does, consisting of a men's washroom on one side and a women's on the other. As their vehicle rolled by, a few ladies would later report, the four of them had caught a glimpse of something they'd all thought truly peculiar.

Right by that shelter house, they would tell police, they had spotted a woman carrying what seemed to be a small child, wrapped in what appeared to be a blanket or a coat. According to the *Evening News*: "Their statements also report that the boy was barefoot and that his legs extending from under the blanket or coat appeared to be bound." The sighting was brief, and none of the women managed to get a good look at the lady's face.

Andy's little body would in fact be found stripped, bound and gagged, so police quickly came to theorize that this shelter house was where all that transpired. After removing everything but his shirt and underwear, Chyrel used a pair of nylon stockings to tie his hands behind his back and another pair to secure his ankles. Lastly, she tied what looked to be a dish towel, possibly intended to be used as a gag, securely around the kid's neck.

About a thousand feet beyond that point was Delaware Park Lake, and a quick, five-minute walk brought them to the northern shore of its easternmost end. Today, the path from that shelter house to the lake is (rudely) interrupted by the Scajaquada Expressway, but in 1961 it was still a straight shot across an open field. Taking Andy and moving dead ahead, Chyrel then began their deliberate march to the water's edge.

It was there, whether on purpose or by horrible accident, that Andy ended up in the water. Presumably thrashing around to the best of his ability, the boy struggled in vain and would soon die of suffocation by drowning. Chyrel, for her part, simply walked away. Amazingly, no one saw a thing.

* * * * * *

BY 6 p.m. Andy had not returned home for supper, and his mother had become concerned.

She went around the corner to the Laux house, her son's stated destination, only to find that no one was home. The family had set off earlier that day on a weekend vacation trip, meaning two full hours had passed since Andy was last seen by anyone. At 6:15 p.m. Francis arrived home from work, and he promptly joined his wife in scouring the neighborhood.

Their effort swiftly became a full-on neighborhood search, with area residents spending the next two hours combing the park and patrolling the adjacent streets. Curiously, Chyrel would later admit to walking right into all the brouhaha. From the *Buffalo Evening News*: "About 7:30 Friday evening, Cheryl told police, she went to the Buffalo Zoo where she talked with a woman near Monkey Island. She recalled their exchanging comments about the missing boy. Cheryl said she then walked along Jewett Pkwy. and noticed a group of people gathered around the Ashley home."

At 8 p.m. Donna contacted the police, frantically telephoning her local precinct to file a missing persons report. An hour later officers were on the scene and questioning neighbors, and their first and only real lead that night came from Edwin Ehrne, who had watched from his porch as Andy was led away and into the zoo. After giving his account to police, Ehrne, wracked with guilt, went out searching for the boy until four o'clock the next morning.

The woman, he'd told them, had been dressed rather nondescriptly, wearing a plain, dark-colored shirt and blouse, with a dark or earth-colored raincoat over top of it. She'd had on shoes with low heels, wore no hat and carried no purse. He approximated her height to be around 5'7" or 5'8" and described her build as "slender." Having only seen her from behind, however, Ehrne was way off with regard to one key detail, and it would taint the whole investigation moving forward. Andy's abductor, he told investigators, had been roughly thirty-five years old.

Police Station No. 17, better known as the Colvin station, was only four blocks from the Ashleys' apartment, just across the northeastern ridge of Delaware Park. At 98 Colvin Avenue, the two-story, no-nonsense brick edifice still stands but is no longer occupied, sitting quietly and in the shadows of the much larger (and still functioning) headquarters of the Buffalo Fire Department's engine 38, seventh battalion stationhouse. Its location, actually, was right up against the New York Central Railroad tracks, not too far from the very spot where Chyrel had taken Ritchie Edgington to play Cowboys and Indians just a day earlier.

There station captain James O'Donnell sprung swiftly into action, calling for an immediate search of the Buffalo Zoo's premises. Daylight was fading fast, but overnight his men were able to inspect its grounds a second time, with the necessary lighting provided by their neighbors at the fire department. By sunrise the next morning, a Saturday, a team of over a hundred police officers had been assembled and a massive search was underway. In addition to his own squad, Captain O'Donnell had called upon members of B district's headquarters and also the crime prevention bureau, as well as about a dozen other auxiliary police officers.

With no luck overnight at the zoo, the hunt was quickly expanded to include all of Delaware Park. At 10 a.m. an underwater recovery unit began dragging Delaware Park Lake, but this initial search turned up nothing. Meanwhile, back at the stationhouse on Colvin Avenue, the skipper was dutifully calling all nearby mental facilities, asking if perhaps any of them had discharged a murderously deranged woman in the past day or so. It was also learned that several busloads of Canadian youths had visited the zoo on Friday, but after checking with immigration authorities police were satisfied that Andy had not wandered aboard one of them.

By 11:15 a.m. a police canine unit was sniffing along the railroad tracks, right in the area where the Edgington kid was claiming he'd been taken to and left tied two days prior. The New York Central Railroad's own police were contributing as well, providing a motorized flatcar outfitted with searchlights that rolled slowly along while officers searched the embankment. Right where those tracks pass the Colvin station, beyond the Nichols School and the Elmwood Franklin School, officers were actually conducting house-to-house searches.

In response to the scandalous 1931 kidnapping and killing of famed aviator Charles Lindbergh's young son, congress had enacted the Federal Kidnapping Act. Also known as the Lindbergh Law, it allows for federal authorities to step in once a child has been missing for twenty-four hours. Accordingly, the FBI showed up at 4 p.m. sharp, installing themselves in the Ashleys' apartment building for the purpose of monitoring incoming phone calls.

So began the frantic search for Andrew Ashley, whose lifeless body lie floating somewhere just beyond the shores of Delaware Park Lake. It would be another day spent looking in vain.

# SIX

## Patty and Elizabeth

A t around the time the FBI was setting up shop at the Ashleys' place on Parkside, Chyrel was a half a mile to the east, out prowling around in the vicinity of her Leroy Avenue home.

Less than a full day had passed since she'd extinguished her first life, and, unbelievably, it seems she was already hungry to recapture whatever sick thrill that depraved action had afforded her. Outrageously, she was wearing a red dress with white polka dots.

It was getting late in the afternoon - a little before 4 p.m., Saturday, June 24 - and Chyrel was just several blocks from home, walking north on Fillmore Avenue in the direction of Main. Near the corner of Wade Avenue, a quiet residential street that runs east off of Fillmore, she happened upon another unaccompanied minor, a little girl outside on her own and possibly ripe for the taking.

Five-year-old Patricia Brown lived with her parents at 2519 Main Street, in the apartment right above the Central Park Grill (opened in 1929, the neighborhood saloon-style tavern is actually one of the oldest in Buffalo and, amazingly, it's still there and open for business). Patty, out exploring the block that passes just behind her building, had been cautioned repeatedly by her parents against talking to strangers. So when Chyrel wandered up, offering to take her to a nearby candy store, the girl had the good sense to get scared and run away.

Within minutes, though, Chyrel spied a second opportunity. Suddenly another little girl, six-year-old Elizabeth Palermo, was out there all by herself, not far from her residence at 2315 Fillmore. The Palermo family's two-story home was right there at the corner of Wade, and Elizabeth's mother was sitting out on her side porch when she happened to look up and catch sight of her daughter in the company of a complete stranger.

"About 4 o'clock I looked up Fillmore and saw my daughter, Elizabeth, hand-in-hand with this older girl," Mrs. Palermo would later tell the *Buffalo Evening News*. "I shouted 'Elizabeth!' and when the older girl heard me she dropped Elizabeth's hand and ran down Fillmore toward Main." A diligent and protective mom, Mrs. Palermo immediately gave chase, losing her along the next block but doubling right back and telephoning the police from back at her house.

Then, while she was waiting to get through, she looked outside to see Chyrel heading right back toward her, having made her way around the block and now approaching from the opposite direction. "While I was waiting on the telephone I saw the girl coming back down Wade," Mrs. Palermo continued. "I didn't even wait for the telephone connection. I dropped the phone and ran after her again. I chased her as she went down Fillmore." Chyrel might have been able to evaded her a second time, too, but just as she was nearing Main a car came rolling up and it drew to a sharp halt right alongside her.

Its driver was Robert Brown, the father of the other little girl Chyrel had attempted to snatch just moments earlier. His daughter Patty had just come rushing in, declaring that a strange lady had tried to lure her away with the promise of some candy. Deciding he'd better go see about this, he had loaded Patty into the car and together they'd gone circling the block, spotting their target just as Mrs. Palermo was losing track of her again. Stepping out of the vehicle, Mr. Brown approached her. "I talked nice to her," he would later tell the *Evening News*. "I wasn't aggravated. I said: 'Why did you want to take my daughter for candy? What's the reason for it?'"

Chyrel replied that she was only out to do a bit of shopping at Hall's Bakery, which seemed plausible because they were standing right out front of its enormous building at 2381 Fillmore. But Mrs. Palermo was rushing toward them, and the moment Chyrel spotted her she bolted off, quickly darting across Main Street and jagging around the corner onto Parker Avenue. Mr. Brown was in hot pursuit, now on foot and shouting ahead for somebody to stop her. Parker almost immediately encounters Amherst Avenue, where two men tried to do just that, but Chyrel went sailing straight past them and right into a house around the corner.

The home there, at 1745 Amherst, was owned by Thomas A. O'Connor, an attorney. Mr. Brown came running up just as the lawyer was stepping outside to see what all the commotion was about, and a patrol car arrived around that same time. Chyrel was taken into custody by police officer Larry Shepperly of the 16th precinct, who wound up turning her over to a pair of plainclothes detectives from the Colvin Avenue stationhouse. That station, of course, was abuzz with activity, with every single officer there almost completely preoccupied with the Ashley kidnapping. A patrol car transported Chyrel there, with the Browns and Mrs. Palermo following behind in Mr. Brown's vehicle.

When questioned by detectives Charles Miller and Joseph Schwartz, Chyrel initially claimed that her name was Michelle Johnson and that she lived at 91 Wade Avenue. Without missing a beat, though, Mrs. Palermo sharply declared, "That's a lie! There's no such number on Wade. It's an empty lot!" She was correct, of course, and, with the exception of some sycamore trees, it still is. "She went white," Mrs. Palermo later told the *Evening News*, recounting Chyrel's reaction to being called out. "She froze. Then she got very excited and began shaking. But she wasn't crying. She seemed upset because she was contradicted."

Mrs. Palermo was asked to leave the room, and after twenty or thirty minutes Chyrel finally came out with her real name. But the top priority at the Colvin station, naturally, was locating three-year-old Andrew Ashley, as well as the mysterious woman who'd taken him a day earlier. And since they believed that woman to be in her thirties, no one really viewed Chyrel as anything other than a fifteen-year-old trouble-maker. Still, Detective Miller would later tell the *Evening News*, when the subject came up she grew "excited and hysterical," adding that "she would repeat, 'Do you think I did this?'"

Ultimately, according to Robert Brown, the detectives told him that Chyrel had "just picked the wrong day to invite children for candy." With that they asked him to drive her home, and Brown would later give the following account to the *Evening News*: "During the trip back she talked a lot but it was a lot of mumbo-jumbo. When we turned at Colvin and Amherst, near the entrance to the Buffalo Zoo, she asked if that was the Zoo and said 'That's where Delaware Park is.' I let her off at Hall's Bakery and cautioned her not to stop and talk to any more youngsters, or offer to buy them candy."

Thomas O'Connor, the attorney whose home Chyrel had come busting into earlier that afternoon, later told the *Evening News* that around 5:15 p.m. his doorbell rang. It was Chyrel, and she wanted to apologize for the big misunderstanding earlier. "She said, 'I want to thank you for being so nice to me. They took me some place where there was a lot of people. Someone there said I wasn't the girl, and they let me go.'" When his wife mentioned something about the Ashley case, Chyrel replied: "Yes, I know. There's a little boy missing. But they're looking for a woman 35, and I'm only 13 years old."

And that, essentially, was the long, tall and short of it. Working with a seriously-flawed description – one that mistook their suspect's age by two full decades – authorities were still far from zeroing in on the kidnapper. They'd had no luck finding Andy, either. An initial drag of Delaware Park Lake had yielded nothing, so there was still hope the boy might be found alive. A team of around two hundred police officers had spent the day probing much of North Buffalo, rechecking the zoo and going over just about every square inch of Delaware Park, including the 269-acre Forest Lawn Cemetery. Nearby Buffalo State College, Buffalo State Hospital (the infamous Richardson Olmstead Complex), Mount Saint Joseph Academy and the LaSalle quarry were also examined thoroughly.

By nightfall the entire city was abuzz, with news of the kidnapping appearing in all the local Saturday papers. The *Buffalo Courier-Express*, out first thing that morning, told of the missing boy as well as the intense search that was underway. The *Buffalo Evening News*, for its part, carried no less than five separate articles, four of them appearing on its front page. Both papers had gotten wind of the Richard Edgington affair, and both were reporting that police believed they had a serial offender on their hands.

The kidnapping of Andrew Ashley was officially a citywide scandal, with parents across the region wide awake to the fact that someone was out there snatching kids, thus far with utter impunity. Neighborhood streets, usually alive on a Saturday night with the sounds of kids out roaming and playing, were unusually quiet that night.

By dawn the next morning – Sunday, June 25 – the number of people searching for the missing Ashley boy had grown to about five hundred. According to the *Courier-Express*, interested parties at that point included "policemen, auxiliary policeman, Boy Scouts, members of the National Guard and volunteer citizens," all of them combing every spot within the vicinity of his disappearance.

Francis and Donna Ashley, meanwhile, were at a complete loss. Donna was a nervous wreck, and an *Evening News* reporter who'd called on them at their apartment found her nearly in shock, chain smoking and wondering aloud how such a thing could happen. "It doesn't seem right," she'd told him. "I have not been able to face the fact. It's something you read about happening to other children… but to have it happen to your own, in your own front yard…"

Chyrel, too, had been captivated by all the newspaper coverage, and as the afternoon wore on she seems to have been thinking an awful lot about the Ashley family. Her uncle, John Palmer, would later report receiving a particularly bizarre phone call from his niece, who jabbered on about the case and even predicted police would probably find the kid floating in the lake at Delaware Park.

Around 1 p.m. she left her home on Leroy, walking a few steps to the corner of Main and entering the Smither-Hill Pharmacy. There, in an act of unbelievable nerve and unspeakable cruelty, she used its phone booth to ring the Ashley residence. It was Donna who answered, and while Chyrel did not identify herself she did have a message for Mrs. Ashley. "Don't worry," she told her. "Your boy is all right. He's here with me. He's OK and isn't hurt. I'll bring him back if you'll call off the police."

That most certainly was not happening. The FBI, in fact, was right there and tracing the call, and soon a pair of agents were on their way to the pharmacy at Main and Leroy. She was long gone by the time they got there, but a clerk remembered a girl using the phone booth earlier, recognizing her as a local who happened to live just around the corner. Moments later, of course, the agents were at the door of 21 Leroy, asking Chyrel a series of questions about the very suspicious phone call she had just placed to the missing boy's poor mother.

Chyrel confessed to making the call, but she claimed to have done so in an effort to bring Mrs. Ashley some measure of comfort, actually. It was a pretty flimsy excuse, but, again, the agents thought they were out there looking for a deranged thirtysomething. Ultimately the two feds chalked it up to an insensitive prank carried out by a thoughtless youth, and with that the name Chyrel Jolls fell off the authorities' radar for a second time.

Then, a little after 2:30 p.m., the call came over the police wire. The body of three-year-old Andrew Ashley had been found, deceased and floating in Delaware Park Lake. He was partially stripped and all tied up. This was no longer a missing persons case. Now it was the gruesome murder of a helpless little boy.

# SEVEN

## "We Are Dealing With A Woman Maniac"

City officials raced to the scene.

Mayor Frank Sedita right away addressed the press, urging parents to keep diligent watch over their kids until police could get a handle on the matter. "We are dealing with a woman maniac," he declared. "Please tell the public to keep a close watch on their children until we apprehend the person responsible fore this horrible crime. Tell them not to let their children out of their sight for a single moment." If Sedita offered any words of comfort or reassurance, those remarks were not reprinted in the *Buffalo Courier-Express*.

Back at the Colvin station, a detective sergeant named Charles Quinn was discussing the case with the precinct's captain, James O'Donnell. Quinn was head of a different squad, the B district headquarters, and he had been working with O'Donnell since the initial Friday night search. Charles DeVoe, captain of the underwater recovery team, soon arrived with the somber news that the deceased body of Andrew Ashley had just been found, noting that his parents needed to be notified before word reached the general public.

Captain O'Donnell assigned the heavy task of informing Mr. and Mrs. Ashley to Detective Quinn. With him Quinn took Lieutenant Milton Speidel, head of the radar squad, who was there working the case on what should have been his day off. Together the two drove over to 195 Jewett Parkway, where the FBI already had an agent stationed in the Ashleys' basement apartment. Quinn and that FBI man had been working this case in tandem, and they had an arrangement with the Ashleys' upstairs neighbors, Mr. and Mrs. Herbert Cloy, to accept personal calls from Quinn on their telephone line.

Quinn and Speidel arrived shortly after 3 p.m., finding the FBI agent already in the Cloys' apartment and awaiting their arrival. A news bulletin had just come across the radio, and when Mrs. Cloy heard it she'd tapped on the floor, their pre-arranged signal for the agent to come upstairs. Gathered together there, Quinn now asked Francis Ashley to politely excuse himself and join them upstairs at the Cloys' apartment.

After delivering Francis the crushing news, along with the revolting circumstances of his boy's discovery, they all made their way downstairs. Francis then took Donna into their bedroom, while the others waited out in the living room. Within moments Donna could be heard wailing in agony, hysterically screaming over and over, "Who killed my baby?" It was a real bad scene. Of the whole grim affair, Quinn told the *Courier-Express* only this: "I had to break the news. I didn't like it."

The job of identifying his son's corpse fell to Francis, so Quinn drove him over to the morgue. They were accompanied by Frank Ellis, Donna's father, who had traveled to Buffalo from Emporium, Pennsylvania, and spent the last forty-some hours keeping sleepless and hopeful vigil alongside his daughter. The Erie County Morgue was located inside the Edward J. Meyer Memorial Hospital, presently known as Erie County Medical Center, near where Kensington Avenue meets Grider Street about a mile to the southeast. Francis was accompanied into the autopsy room by the Reverend Daniel Kennedy, who had earlier prayed over and blessed the boy's remains at the scene of his discovery.

Back home, Donna Ashley was inconsolable, and in describing her condition the papers used the word "prostrated" a lot. A physician had been summoned, and he'd arrived around 3:25 p.m. to administer a strong sedative, then ordering her to bed. Leaving the Ashleys' apartment he told the *Courier-Express* that, given the circumstances, she was "doing remarkably well." A pastor from Donna's church, St. Mark Church on Woodward Avenue, was also there to sit with her awhile, and on his way out he characterized her as "very brave."

The Ashley place, according to the *Courier-Express*, was promptly descended upon by curious onlookers from all over the city: "Families, including children, came in cars. Others walked by and looked in at the apartment building. Boys came on bicycles. Auxiliary policemen, assigned to the vicinity, kept everyone moving." A few hours later Donna emerged, speaking briefly with the *Buffalo Evening News* and stating only the following: "Everybody did all they could. We are grateful. I'd like to thank everyone who helped in the search."

Police, meanwhile, had no new promising leads or clues pointing them to the killer's identity, and they were working only with what they had – an inaccurate description and a list of suspects they had already ruled out. Wondering if they might have missed something, the detectives started revisiting the names of those they'd already questioned, and at around 5:30 p.m. Chyrel was brought into the Colvin station for a second interview.

She wasn't happy about it, either. Detective Schwartz, who had dealt with Chyrel just the day before, again reported that she was "very belligerent" right off the bat. When questioned directly about Andrew Ashley's murder, he told the *Evening News*, she denied any part of it, exclaiming "check my record" repeatedly. In fact, Chyrel told detectives, she was on the lookout for this woman herself. "She said she was going to find her and was going to kill her before she got her aunt's baby," Schwartz explained.

Chyrel was bizarre as all hell, Schwartz would have to admit, but police simply could not see beyond the fact that she was little more than a child herself. So, for the third time in just two days, the name Chyrel Jolls was written off, and once again the officers cut her loose.

Shortly before 6 p.m., Erie County Medical Examiner James Creighton announced that he had completed the boy's autopsy. It was his opinion that Andrew Ashley had perished by suffocation, secondary to drowning. This meant he had not been strangled beforehand, and the implication was that he'd been tied up and tossed into Delaware Park Lake while he was still alive. Creighton added that it was not his opinion that the boy had been molested prior to his death.

He approximated the time of death to be somewhere between 5 p.m. and 5:30 p.m. Friday, within an hour or so of the kid's abduction. "It is a sight like this that makes my job difficult," Creighton told the *Courier-Express* shortly after revealing his findings. "When you see a child brutally murdered, it tears your heart out."

Back at the city's police headquarters, located downtown at the southwest corner of Church and Franklin Streets, Buffalo Police Commissioner Frank N. Felicetta was strategizing like mad. The title of commissioner, generally, belongs to a police force's top and most respected cop. Felicetta had indeed dedicated his whole life to law enforcement, and as a veteran officer he'd garnered a reputation as something of a stickler for the rule of law (years later, in response to accusations of officers engaging in police brutality, he famously made sixty-two of his own men stand in a lineup). Now, as the face of this investigation, he was doggedly evaluating the case from all angles.

The FBI, on the other hand, was packing up and heading back to Washington. Now that the Ashley boy's body had been recovered and listed as deceased, it was no longer a kidnapping and therefore no longer a federal concern. Now it was a local matter, one to be handled between the city of Buffalo and its people, who were growing increasingly uneasy over the female lunatic out there on the loose and meddling with toddlers, probably already in search of her next victim.

\* \* \* \* \* \*

THERE were no new developments the next day, Monday. There was some women's clothing and a fifteen-foot extension cord found by Delaware Park Lake, but nothing would ever come of it. Investigators were still grappling there, hoping to find Andrew's missing articles of clothing, and they were doing the same in Forest Lawn Cemetery's several small, breathtakingly calm and serene ponds.

Police also revisited Chyrel's two earlier victims, Richard Edgington and Susan Benedict, bringing them to various North Buffalo homes so they could have a look at some area suspects. Chyrel was not among them, and neither Ritchie nor Susie were able to be of much help to investigators on this occasion. At the Colvin station, meanwhile, the telephones were ringing off the hook with concerned citizens phoning in bits of information, and Commissioner Felicetta commented to the *Buffalo Courier-Express* that none of these were being ignored or overlooked.

That evening, police released to the public their working description of the killer. From the *Buffalo Evening News*: "Age 35 to 40. Height about 5 feet 6 inches. Blue eyes. Brown hair with streaks of gray, although some reports say her hair is black. High cheek bones, smooth skin." That paper's own artist, Bruce Shanks, drew up a sketch based on that description, but his initial rendering, frankly, looks a lot less like Chyrel Jolls and more like a young Donald Trump all duded up for a hunting retreat.

On its front page, the *Evening News* even posted notice of a $1,000 reward for information leading to the killer's arrest and conviction. Predictably, the *Courier-Express* issued a near-identical one the following morning. The *Courier-Express* urged its readers to provide any relevant information to the police, while the *Evening News* called for all tips to be phoned into its crime desk.

The following day, Tuesday, consisted largely of following up on and sifting through the numerous tips that came flooding in. Three boys playing on Elmwood Avenue reported seeing, from the bridge where that street crosses over Scajaquada Creek, what they interpreted as a woman's body floating in in the water below. The underwater recovery team was dispatched to the spot at once, but their search revealed only a plastic white baseball bat.

Police were also checking the files of area psychiatric facilities, with emphasis on the medical records of recently-discharged women under the age of fifty. They even employed a bit of cutting-edge technology, a computer, to sift through all that raw data and flag all patients with files containing the name "Johnson" and/or the numbers "229." Their killer, they knew, had told Richard Edgington to use the name "Davie Johnson" if asked, and she'd told Susan Benedict her house number was 2290. North Buffalo postal workers were also asked to keep an eye out for these same two indicators.

Commissioner Felicetta was directing officers citywide to halt and question every female matching the description issued earlier, and eleven separate women had been picked up on that day alone. After being brought in and questioned for a short while, each of these ladies had promptly been released. To that end, and with no better options, police also were still rechecking and following up on some of the persons of interest they'd already cleared or written off. One of those names belonged to Chyrel Jolls, and this would mark her third occasion being interrogated by detectives at the Colvin station.

Investigators had arranged to have both Richard Edgington and Susan Benedict have a look at her, but, interestingly, neither were able to positively identify Chyrel as their abductor. Captain O'Donnell would later provide the *Evening News* with the following explanation: "When the Jolls girl was viewed by the two children, she was wearing her hair in pony style and looked like a girl of 13. The children as well as two other adult witnesses said she was not the suspected abductor."

Walking out of the stationhouse that evening, Chyrel might have felt downright invincible. Or, she may have (correctly) sensed that the walls were rapidly closing in and that her capture was imminent. Either way, she spent the remainder of the week laying low.

## "We Are Dealing With A Woman Maniac"

* * * * * *

WEDNESDAY, June 28, was the day of Andrew Ashley's funeral. He was laid to rest not in Buffalo, but in his parents' former home of Le Roy, where he was interred at St. Francis Cemetery.

Investigators, meanwhile, were casting a wide net, expanding the parameters of their search well beyond the North Buffalo area. A Canadian woman, based on her appearance, was detained all the way up in in Niagara Falls (the American side), and as far west as Erie, Pennsylvania, authorities were hassling some poor woman for the same reason. All Buffalo area candy vendors were provided with flyers urging them to keep vigilant, as the unknown offender was known to chomp on hard candy as she lured her victims to their fate.

Curiously, police did receive a report of some Chyrel-like activity later that day. From the *Buffalo Evening News*: "Late Wednesday afternoon, two young girls reported a woman at Elmwood Ave. and West Delavan St. had invited one of them to go to the zoo. Again, police cars failed to locate the woman."

The next day investigators were back at Delaware Park Lake, combing the terrain around the spot where Andrew's body had been discovered. While grappling in the water that afternoon, right by the spot where he'd been found, investigators located the boy's olive-colored pants, as well as a tied-up plastic bag that may have been used in his attempted suffocation. "The knotted plastic bag and the checkered trousers," the *Buffalo Courier-Express* reported, "were located only a few feet from where the boy's body, clad only in a tee-shirt and undershorts, was found five days ago."

Aerial photos taken the day before had also given investigators a fresh perspective. From the air, the boorish manner in which the recently-constructed Scajaquada Expressway interrupts the park became obvious for the first time. Ending at Delaware Avenue, right by the lake, the expressway's off ramp formed a huge loop which caused that area to be cut off to foot traffic and therefore overlooked almost entirely. It was the spot just southwest of the shelter house, within a few hundred yards of where the body had been found.

There workers located a patch of vegetation that was all matted down, as if someone had rested there awhile, and nearby they found three or four strips of torn toweling that appeared to match the fabric tied around Andy's body. This was quickly determined to be from "commercial toweling," likely the type that rolls out of a wall dispenser, so police asked workers of facilities that had those to report any damaged or missing fabric. Laundry service workers were also asked to keep an eye out for the same thing along their routes.

Police had also managed to find Richard Edgington's pith helmet. The thing had been discovered in some brush alongside the New York Central Railroad tracks, about a quarter mile east of where the kid had been left tied, seemingly an indication that Chyrel had discarded it thoughtlessly on her walk back home. Inspecting it closely, a detective sergeant named Frank Angelo of the night squad discovered five strands of hair - brunette, eleven inches long and almost certainly belonging to a woman. Immediately they were sent to an FBI lab in Washington for the 1961 version of forensic analysis.

That evening, via the *Evening News*, police released a revised description of their killer:

- HEIGHT – Minimum, 5 feet 4 inches; maximum, 5 feet 6 inches; most probably 5 feet 5 inches.

- AGE – Minimum 25, maximum 35; most probably, 29 to 31.
- WEIGHT – 115 to 130 pounds; stockily built, but not heavy.
- COMPLEXION – Dark; some witnesses say she appeared to have a good suntan; clear, smooth skin.
- HAIR – Described variously as "dirty" blonde, light brown, brown with reddish cast and dark brown; cut short or about neck length; could be parted in the middle or worn in pony tail; on June 22, she was wearing her hair with a short pony tail through a metal ring.
- POSTURE – Walks straight and upright and "with a solid step."
- GENERAL APPEARANCE – Face is thin, oblong with well-defined cheekbones; short neck and short waist; legs described as "heavy calfed," but "shapely."

Alongside it the paper ran an updated composite sketch, again drawn by their in-house cartoonist Bruce Shanks. Shanks' talents had been commissioned by the commissioner himself, Frank Felicetta, who had provided the artist with fresh details gleaned from the ongoing questioning of witnesses. Among them were people who had seen Chyrel with one or the other of her victims, as well as two of those victims themselves. Susan Benedict and Richard Edgington, Chyrel's first two abductees, each were shown Shanks' new drawing, and both gave the thumbs up prior to its release to the public.

Upon further questioning, in fact, five-year-old Susan Benedict had provided investigators with at least one crucial piece of intel. While out driving with her mother, about two weeks after her brief abduction, Susie claimed she'd seen her kidnapper walking into a store along Fillmore Avenue. This revelation shifted to the focus of the investigation to the Fillmore-Leroy district, and now a seven-man squad was going house-to-house within three blocks of Chyrel's home.

Richard Edgington was being pumped for additional information as well, and on Sunday he and his mother (and a photographer from the *Courier-Express*) accompanied investigators as they retraced the route of his kidnapping. Setting off around 1 p.m., a three-man detail – comprised of Assistant Detective Chief John McCarthy, Lieutenant John Dugan and Detective Gerald Dove – escorted Ritchie as he led them from his home to the zoo. Along the way the kid recalled and revealed the two occasions on which Chyrel had paused to interact with strangers, and police were now pleading for those strangers to come forward. Not one of them would.

Once inside the zoo Ritchie recognized a few things here and there, but by and large his attention was waning. Outside its gates, though, he recognized groundskeeper Sam Costa, saying to his chaperones, "that is the man who hollered at the lady because we were walking on the grass." They'd been out there for nearly an hour and a half, and Ritchie was quickly becoming exhausted. Detectives McCarthy and Dove took turns carrying him, either piggyback or on their shoulders, but around 2:20 p.m. it started to rain and the mission was called off for the day. Plans were made to resume the following day at 1 p.m.

Chyrel, at around this time, was back in the North Park neighborhood, meandering along Parkside near its intersection with Tacoma, a block north of Hertel. At one point a passing motorist, Frederick Goldstein, noticed something odd – it was Chyrel, whipping a tree trunk with a branch she'd torn off the tree. Goldstein, who lived six blocks away on Covington Road, was out driving with his son Phillip, a college student. Phillip, upon spotting her, pointed out her striking resemblance to the newly-released sketch of the woman who had the whole city on edge.

When they saw Chyrel step aboard a southbound bus, the Goldsteins decided to trail behind it in their vehicle. She got off at Main and Harvard Place, Frederick later told the *Courier-Express,* and when she spotted the father-son team she approached and confronted them straight away. "She came up to us and asked, 'Are you following me?'" the elder Goldstein recalled. "I asked her if there was any reason she should be afraid she was being followed and she answered, 'No, and unless you're cops, be on your way.'"

Goldstein, apparently, then informed her that he and his son were on official business, acting in their capacity as private investigators (it was a total lie; the 42-year-old was actually a small business owner, and his 21-year-old son was a pre-med student at the University of Buffalo). With that they were able to get Chyrel to give them her name and her address, which Fred Goldstein reported to the Colvin station later that evening. There, however, he was told that a girl by that name had already been questioned and cleared on more than one occasion.

It was a full week into the investigation, and police were working around the clock. The eighty officers assigned to the case were working twelve-hour shifts, and they were still without a solid lead. Around two thousand tips had been phoned in, and while all were run down none of them really bore fruit. And while the name Chyrel Jolls had come up over and over and over again, detectives on each occasion had been blinded by her youth. Tellingly, however, Commissioner Felicetta did make this statement to the *Evening News*: "I am fearful that we may have talked to this woman and passed her by."

It wasn't just the newspapers carrying incessant coverage of the case. Television, a comparatively new medium, was in healthy competition with print media in terms of bringing folks their news, and the evening newscast had already become a regular part of the middle-class American routine. Local station WGR-TV, broadcast on channel two, ran a program that evening featuring a panel of guests that "analyzed aspects of the Ashley crime," as the *Courier-Express* put it.

One of those guests was a Yale-educated psychiatrist and physician named Samuel Yochelson, and his comments on the matter were mellower in nature and from a decidedly gentler perspective. From the *Courier-Express*: "Dr. Yochelson emphasized the fact that the woman involved in the crimes was sick and needed help and that it was his duty to see that she received help." Yochelson was the medical director of the Jewish Family Service of Buffalo, and he maintained his own psychiatric practice downtown.

One viewer, watching from her home, was especially taken by Dr. Yochelson's remarks. Coming from her TV screen she heard, for the first time since the investigation began, the voice of a medical professional calling not for her capture and imprisonment, but for this troubled and unknown person to finally be heard and understood. She thought Dr. Yochelson was nice. Chyrel would, in fact, later tell police that she'd been "impressed."

# EIGHT

## Another Look

C hyrel Jolls had already been picked up and questioned by police three times, and she'd fooled them on every occasion. Independent of all that, she had even outsmarted the FBI.

But now, with public pressure mounting and their investigation really at a standstill, police were doing what the *Buffalo Evening News* called a "routine checkback," reinterviewing previously-cleared subjects in hopes of catching something they might have overlooked. And, with the investigation entering its tenth full day, extra manpower was still urgently being funneled into the effort.

There were fifty or so women who needed to be reinterviewed, and members of the auto theft and robbery squad were assigned to the task, working out of the Colvin station. It was the head of that squad, Lieutenant Thomas Hennessey, who noticed that one name in particular stood out. Chyrel Jolls had been hauled into that very station three times already, all within the context of this same investigation, and on each occasion her behavior had been noted as unusual. The age difference was striking, alright, but certainly these factors alone warranted further attention.

It was around 11 a.m. on Monday, July 3, when Lieutenant Hennessey arrived at 21 Leroy Avenue. Chyrel was at home, and Hennessey told her parents she needed to come down to the stationhouse and answer a few questions. Georgia, her mother, gave her consent – Chyrel was just fifteen years old, legally a minor – and with that Hennessey drove her back to the Colvin station.

Once again, Chyrel flat-out denied any involvement in the killing of Andrew Ashley. She did, however, surprise her interrogators with an odd request: she asked to meet with Dr. Samuel Yochelson, whom she had seen the night before on channel two discussing the case. "She explained she had seen him on a Sunday television program about the Ashley case, and thought he was nice," Commissioner Felicetta told the *Evening News*. Correctly sensing that they were onto something, he quickly set up a meeting with Yochelson, who had an office downtown in the Sidway Building at 775 Main Street.

Hennessey drove Chyrel over there, arriving around 2:30 p.m., and she and Dr. Yochelson spoke privately for several hours. Confidentiality laws prevent us from knowing exactly what transpired, but clearly Yochelson, upon concluding his initial examination, did indicate to Hennessey that there was significant cause for concern with respect to this young girl.

That bit of information took the Colvin station by storm, and right away the place came alive with a rejuvenated energy and purpose. Their entire investigation, basically, now consisted of finding out more about Chyrel Jolls.

Around 5 p.m. she was brought back to the stationhouse, with Dr. Yochelson also on the scene to provide whatever assistance he could. Arrangements had already been made for both Richard Edgington and Susan Benedict to be brought back in, as police were hoping another look at Chyrel might jog something in their memories. They had each viewed her the previous Tuesday, but neither of them had been able to identify Chyrel as their abductor on that occasion. However, Captain James O'Donnell would later remark to the *Evening News*, at that time "she was wearing her hair in pony style and looked like a girl of 13." Now, with her hair done up in a French roll, "the Jolls girl looked entirely different," and much more mature in appearance.

Five-year-old Ritchie Edgington, actually, had been out with detectives all afternoon, and he'd just completed a second day of being trotted around Delaware Park and having his memory probed. Chyrel was standing outside the Colvin station, flanked by several police officers, when the cop car he was riding in pulled up to the building. Stepping out of the vehicle, Detective Joseph Schwartz would later tell the *Evening News*, the boy cried, "That's the woman there. She's the one..."

Inside, Chyrel did agree to appear in a lineup. A change of clothes was retrieved from her home – a blue and gray plaid dress, a gray corduroy coat and gray high-heeled shoes – and three other women, local volunteers, had agreed to appear alongside her. According to the *Evening News*: "The group appeared on the showup stage twice, each time in different order, to doublecheck any identifications." And this time, under that specific set of circumstances, both Richard Edgington and Susan Benedict did positively identify Chyrel as their abductor.

At some point Dr. Yochelson ushered both Chyrel and Ritchie into the same room, opening up a dialogue between them, with Commissioner Felicetta observing silently. And, Felicetta later told the *Evening News*, not once did the kid sway from his earlier proclamation that Chyrel had been his abductor. "You took my helmet," he exclaimed, then adding, "You took me." Still Chyrel denied all of this, and Dr. Yochelson allowed her to retort. "Then," Felicetta said, "she began a cross-examination of him that was just as good as an attorney would do. But she couldn't shake him."

Chyrel's interrogators couldn't really shake her, either. "She says she loves children," Felicetta told the *Buffalo Courier-Express*, "and wouldn't do anything to harm them." Members of law enforcement, on the other hand, were an entirely different matter. "She says she hates policemen," he added, "and said 'those dirty cops are always following me and bothering me.'" Obviously, Chyrel was combative. At some point she even stated that she'd shot a cop when she was eight years old and living in the little town of Dayton. What's more, he said, "the girl continually lashed out at newspaper reporters and photographers, voicing a threat to several of the photographers, 'to break your camera if you take a picture.'"

And, when presented with photographs of Andrew Ashley's little drowned body, Chyrel's reaction was awfully curious. From the *Evening News*: "After looking through the file, she turned her gaze toward her questioners and declared: 'What do you expect me to do – jump up and down?'" In all her hubris, though, Chyrel did allow investigators to collect from her a hair sample, providing them with several strands she plucked from her head right then and there. The FBI lab in Washington already had the strands of hair found in the pith helmet, and these were rushed there for forensic comparison.

John Palmer, Chyrel's uncle on nearby Tacoma Avenue, arrived at the Colvin station as soon as he heard that his niece was being held there. Upon learning the reason for her detainment, and sitting down with her face-to-face, Palmer became overwhelmed and broke down in tears. Recalling her phone call to him a little over a week earlier, in which Chyrel had offhandedly predicted that the Ashley boy would turn up in Delaware Park Lake, Palmer wept as he asked her how she could have possibly known that. Emphatically and re-peatedly, Chyrel insisted, "I didn't kill him, I didn't kill him."

Georgia arrived shortly after midnight, while Chyrel was being in-terviewed again by Dr. Yochelson. An hour later Yochelson emerged, declaring it his professional opinion that the girl required a full-scale psychological evaluation at nearby Meyer Memorial Hospital, so Georgia signed the parental consent paperwork. Her father Howard, on the other hand, was conspicuously absent, as Felicetta indicat-ed to the *Courier-Express*. "Although she was here for several hours Monday, and until almost three [the following] morning," he noted, "Chyrel's father never came to Police Headquarters to enquire, or to aid her."

Certainly, Commissioner Felicetta allowed, Chyrel Jolls was "a prime suspect" in the kidnapping and the killing of three-year-old Andrew Ashley. Still, he reminded the press, police were "by no means positive she is guilty." But the entire city of Buffalo had been on edge for over a week and a half, and now it wanted answers. Its journalists, then, will have to be forgiven for having run rather roughshod over the accused's presumption of innocence.

\* \* \* \* \* \*

A thorough search of Chyrel's home, executed earlier in the evening, had netted a fascinating array of clues and several bits of evidence, although much of it largely circumstantial at best. Led by arresting officer Thomas Hennessey, the toss of the Jolls' apartment quickly turned up a set of clothing matching the description of the outfit worn by the "woman" who'd taken Andrew Ashley. Those were taken into evidence, as was every other item or article that could possibly be considered of interest or germane to the investigation.

Among them were two sheets of paper, which the *Buffalo Courier-Express* described as being "of the type used by school children for compositions," which seemed to comprise a brief, hastily-assembled makeshift diary covering the past month or so. "It's really more just a batch of notes," Commissioner Felicetta told the paper. "They contain random jottings about her activities during the last few weeks with several references to the Ashley murder."

Under the heading, "An account of my life… and why I do things," Chyrel admitted, for instance, to calling "the home of the Ashilys" on the day their boy's body was discovered. Still, she maintained, she was a "good girl" who "would even die" to prove it. "She has a tremendous memory and a vivid imagination," Felicetta remarked, "but she doesn't spell well at all."

Even more significantly, detectives found amongst her things a crudely-drawn map that, out of context at least, certainly looked to be an evidential jackpot. Drawn on light blue paper, it depicted the area around the zoo from overhead, shown south to north and bisected vertically by Parkside Avenue. Purporting to illustrate the route Chyrel had taken while out strolling on June 23, the day of Andrew's vanishing, the map was titled - right up top, written neatly and in cursive - "The way I went last Friday."

According to that sketch, written in her own hand, Chyrel had left home that day and walked three blocks down Main before turning right onto Florence Avenue, entering Delaware Park where that street ended at Parkside. It's not really drawn proportionally, but, via a solid line marked "Going," the map suggests she then made her way onto the "gofe feiled" before heading to the zoo and passing by the "Monkey Place." At that point she exited the park, the line indicating her path now marked "Way Back Home" and travelling up West Oakwood Place (spelled "Ockwood") to Main. Delaware Park Lake, however, was nowhere to be found on that map.

And then there were the newspaper clippings. In addition to the numerous articles covering the Ashley case, police found a couple of images that concerned them especially, which the *Courier-Express* described thusly: "Two color pictures, clipped from a brush company catalogue, were found in Chyrel's room. The pictures portrayed a man washing a baby in a small tub, and another domestic scene with a father and an infant." It was all pretty spooky, especially given the circumstances.

Investigators also took note of a book Chyrel owned called *Claudia and David*, a 1943 young adult novel written by the author Rose Franken. On its first page, the *Buffalo Evening News* reported, was scrawled the following declaration: "This book is my book to tell how I feel." It was the second in a series of books centering around the fictional Claudia and David Naughton, a young married couple living in Connecticut with their two boys, Bobby and Matthew. According to the *Courier-Express*, police found "several marked passages about people falling into water and drowning, and several more notations about strangulation using a plastic bag."

Also confiscated were a pair of letters, one Chyrel had received and one she was in the process of writing. The former was from the young man she'd been dating up until the previous month, and his letter shed some light not only on their recent breakup, but also on Chyrel's activities the day after Andrew Ashley had gone missing. It began: "I was thinking of what you said Saturday and I think you were right about us. So I am writing this letter to tell you that I will not bother you any more and do as you said, find another girl."

That Saturday, it seems, the two of them had gone for a walk in the Parkside neighborhood and ended up by the park, tracing its perimeter while formally dissolving their relationship. The boy, whose name police declined to release to the public, had escorted Chyrel on a dozen or so dates over the previous five months, although nothing in his letter, dated June 27, really suggested he was all that upset about their breakup. "You are right about we are two different type of persons and won't mix," he instead conceded.

Using the return address on the letter's envelope, police tracked the kid down at his home on Hertel Avenue. A pair of homicide bureau detectives were dispatched there, and he seems to have cooperated gladly and in full, walking the men through the brief teenage romance he'd shared with their alleged murderess. She had acted "disturbed" that Saturday, he told them. And, when they'd come across a police car and a crowd searching for the missing Ashley boy, Chyrel had seemed awfully keen to get involved.

"He said Cheryl stopped to ask someone in the group if there were any new developments in the search for the boy," the *Evening News* would later report. "As they strolled on, the boy recalled, she declared, 'I hope they get the person who did it because I'm afraid.'" In that letter the boy also had enclosed a necklace, which police noted did not turn up in their search of Chyrel's residence.

## Another Look

The other letter, the one Chyrel started but never finished, spoke volumes. Addressed to what the *Courier-Express* referred to as an "unidentified clergyman," the letter began: "Dear Rev. .........., I am writing because I am in trouble and would like to talk..."

.

# NINE

## A Reluctant Confession

A t 462 Grider Street, on the city's east side and just beyond the Fillmore-Leroy district, stood the Edward J. Meyer Memorial Hospital, on the grounds of what is today called Erie County Medical Center. Opened in 1918 as Buffalo City Hospital, the facility had since been renamed after Edward Meyer, a physician there who had served as the first president of its board of managers. Today much of the campus is occupied by parking and other hospital buildings, but in 1961 most of that space was still a beautiful, recuperative open-air garden, in place to promote a tranquil recovery.

Arriving there in the earliest hours of Tuesday morning – it was the Fourth of July, Independence Day, ironically – Chyrel was checked in and processed for housing in Building K, the hospital's recently-constructed psychiatric ward. Patients there were not confined to their beds, or even to their rooms. They dressed in street clothes, mingled and ate with one another and roamed the halls basically as free as they pleased, prevented only from wandering floor to floor or beyond the building's locked doors.

The next day Georgia came to visit, bringing along her own sister Estelle Ott, Chyrel's aunt from over the border in Welland. Chyrel, her mother would later report, seemed "very upset" during their visit, at one point telling Georgia flatly, "Now I've hurt you, and you must be mad at me." Georgia assured her she was not, and before she and Estelle left the hospital Chyrel made a singular request: she wanted her mother to call on Dr. Yochelson, with whom she felt uniquely at ease, and ask him to visit her at Meyer Memorial. Confused but willing to do whatever she could to help her daughter in crisis, Georgia agreed.

Howard Jolls, on the other hand, seemed to be dealing with the stressful unpleasantness by withdrawing from the world outside the family's apartment nearly altogether. When a reporter for the *Buffalo Evening News* stopped by that afternoon, Howard spoke to him only through a partially-opened door, firmly declaring he didn't appreciate the recent media attention, nor the "parade of cars" that had been lining up to get a look at 21 Leroy ever since the papers revealed that to be his daughter's address.

The resultant article, published that evening, painted a grim portrait of a sad and shell-shocked ne'er-do-well, out of work and wrestling chronically with intemperance, sitting all day in a "blue chair by the window" with the "television set turned loud – drowning out the thoughts in his mind." Like his wife, Howard was convinced of his daughter's innocence, telling the reporter, "I know she is emotional. But I can't believe this thing of her." What's more, he said, he was concerned for his family's already-bleak future. "Will I be able to get a job again?" he wondered aloud. "What about my other children? What will happen to us?"

That afternoon, shortly after Georgia and Estelle got back, another reporter had arrived, this one from the *Buffalo Courier-Express*. Georgia agreed to speak with him, and while she declined to say much about the visit she'd just had with Chyrel, she did give a brief rundown of her daughter's various behavioral difficulties. "I've said there was something wrong with Chyrel for ten years," she boldly declared. Still, she added, "I just can't bring myself to believe she did this."

Howard echoed his wife's sentiment, although, interestingly, he did allow that he had sensed something wasn't right ever since the FBI had come by looking for Chyrel a good nine days earlier. In saying so, actually, Howard provided what would be the article's most titillating bit of information: "I tried to pump it out of her," he said. "She told me a few things, but there was quite a lot she was covering up." When asked what that might be, Howard simply got up and left the room.

Investigators, meanwhile, were spending what should have been a fine summer holiday working tirelessly, interviewing a slew of witnesses and generally building their case against Chyrel Jolls. Estelle Ott, her aunt, told them of the time she'd tied her young son up in a back room and then reported him missing. Police also took statements from Elizabeth Hylant, who signed an affidavit saying she'd watched from her workplace as Chyrel had walked off with Richard Edgington on June 22, as well as from a few kids who knew Chyrel from school, claiming to have seen her with Ritchie on the tracks that day. They also spoke with a man named Theodore LaVigna, a department store salesman from nearby Tonawanda, who claimed to have seen Chyrel with Andrew Ashley near Delaware Park Lake around 4:30 p.m. on June 23, the day he'd vanished.

And, later that day, word came back from the FBI: the strands of hair found in the Edgington kid's helmet were most likely a match for those known to have come from the head of their prime suspect. It was Detective Chief John Whalen, who had been helping oversee the investigation, who made the announcement to the press, confidently telling the *Evening News*: "The hairs from the helmet match those of Cheryl Jolls when microscopically compared. The hairs from the helmet are those of Cheryl Jolls or those of someone else with the same characteristics."

The likelihood of "someone else with the same characteristics" leaving her hair in Ritchie's helmet was laughably slim, of course. Still, Whalen allowed, they would test them against the hair of Ritchie Edgington's mother and grandmother, simply for the avoidance of all doubt. "I am sure we will receive negative reports," Whalen predicted. "That is, no matching characteristics."

Investigators now had Chyrel firmly in their crosshairs, and the following morning's *Courier-Express* duly noted that they were taking the FBI's report "as further evidence in their case against the 15-year-old North Buffalo girl."

\* \* \* \* \* \*

As the sun came up the next morning Detective Chief Whalen was still at his desk working diligently, drawing up paperwork to take into court that afternoon. He, like most of his men, was thoroughly exhausted. The 34-year-old father of five had been working this case around the clock for twelve straight days, and he was not about to stop now. Or so he thought. When he collapsed in his office from sheer fatigue, though, Whalen was taken home and forced to endure at least a day's respite.

He had attended, just the night before, a meeting between police officials and the district attorney's office, called to strategize how best to prosecute this remarkably unusual case. The Erie County District Attorney, at that time, was Carman F. Ball, then in his first term and known mostly for his focus on white collar crime. This case was an entirely different animal, and 1961 was, after all, an election year (Ball would go on to win his re-election, and two years later he would be appointed to the New York State Supreme Court; it was Justice Ball, in fact, who would preside over the years-long investigation into the 1971 Attica prison riots).

They'd convened in Ball's office at the Erie County Courthouse, at 25 Delaware Avenue, just across Church Street from police head-quarters downtown. The city had two kidnappings and a murder on its hands, and no one doubted that Chyrel was responsible for all of it. Proving that in court, however, was another matter. After three and a half hours spent assessing all the evidence they'd gathered so far, it was decided that the best approach was to begin by charging Chyrel with the Edgington crime alone. District Attorney Ball explained things to the *Buffalo Courier-Express*: "In the cases involving the killing of Andrew Ashley and the kidnapping of Susan Benedict, I advised them (the police officials) that at this stage of the investigation I do not feel there is sufficient evidence to secure a warrant for her arrest."

Later that Thursday morning, then, Assistant Detective Chief John McCarthy walked into Buffalo's City Court building, at that time located just across the street at 42 Delaware Avenue. He was accompanied by Lieutenant Thomas Hennessey, as well as a slew of witnesses ready to attest to the statements they'd given to police. After formally applying to the city clerk for a kidnapping warrant, the matter was then heard by the Honorable Casimer T. Partyka, an acting chief justice with Buffalo City Court. Partyka, however, ruled that his courtroom lacked the jurisdiction to prosecute a minor when a death is not involved. Instead, Partyka said, "This matter should be taken up in Children's Court or presented directly to the grand jury."

The courts weren't the only ones all hung up on formality. The local chapter of the American Civil Liberties Union, the Niagara Frontier Branch, had chimed in that afternoon, chastising local police for what they viewed as an infringement on Chyrel's constitutional right to due process. In an official statement, the organization decried not only "the lack of propriety on the part of the Buffalo Police Department in the handling of the chief suspect in the case," but also the rabid sensationalism that pervaded local media coverage.

The papers had been making all kinds of hay, alright, and the ACLU, those fuddy-duddies, pointed out that "the suspect has already been tried in the communication media of the community." What's more, they said, there was "no justification for the detailed exposure of the suspect's background before the indictment or warrant for arrest was recommended by the district attorney."

And while the Supreme Court case mandating the Miranda warning was still five years off, the ACLU did point out that Chyrel lacked proper legal representation, and that there was no indication she had been advised of her right to obtain it. There was no money for a lawyer, of course. But an acquaintance of the Jolls family, an attorney named Louis Robert Leisner, did agree to handle the matter free of charge. Leisner, 33, was from Gowanda, so Howard and Georgia likely knew him from their time in Cattaraugus County. He agreed to visit Chyrel at Meyer Memorial later that evening.

Around 1 p.m. Georgia made her way downtown, calling on Dr. Yochelson at his office and passing along her daughter's urgent request that he call on her at the hospital. Under the circumstances, the 55-year-old psychiatrist could hardly say no; Chyrel was refusing to speak with anyone besides himself, and an entire city was loudly demanding answers only she could provide. Georgia signed the requisite paperwork, making Dr. Yochelson her daughter's personal physician, and he agreed to go see her that evening.

Yochelson arrived at the hospital around 6:30 p.m. to find Georgia already there waiting for him, as well as Commissioner Felicetta, who escorted him to Chyrel's room so he could consult with his patient in private. He and Chyrel spoke at length, quietly and in measured tones, almost certainly a technique to make her feel at ease and comfortable enough to open up. Finally, after about two full hours, it worked. Regarding three-year-old Andrew Ashley, Chyrel confessed to taking him, leading him to the edge of Delaware Park Lake and leaving him tied on the shore. She stopped short of admitting to his killing, though, claiming the boy had been alive when she'd left him.

Yochelson called Georgia into the room, and Chyrel repeated her confession. Then, with both Chyrel and her mother's consent, he called in Commissioner Felicetta, who listened as his prime suspect at last took responsibility for Andrew Ashley's disappearance. She then broke down and began sobbing, Felicetta later told the *Buffalo Evening News*, expressing remorse for the boy's parents and asking to see them in person. "She wanted to express her sorrow to them," he said. "She is truly remorseful now and cried when she told me about the cases." With that they all decided to let Chyrel get a good night's sleep, and that further questioning would resume the next day.

It was a watershed moment in the investigation, for sure. But even as Chyrel was giving and repeating her confession, something interesting was happening just outside Building K at the hospital's main gate. L. Robert Leisner, her attorney, had arrived around 7:30 p.m., but he had been denied access by the hospital's administration. What's more, Georgia later told the *Evening News*, she had requested Leisner's presence during the confession and had been flat-out denied.

In a legal petition filed in response to that incident, Leisner quite plainly stated his client's case: "The child, Chyrel Jolls, gravely ill, without counsel, facing the most serious criminal charges, is alone in the hospital without legal protection, making statements to the police and others, by persuasion, direction and lead, while thus deprived of all legal help."

# TEN

## Proceedings

Having had no luck at Buffalo City Court, District Attorney Carman Ball decided on Friday, July 7, to file a warrant application with Erie County Court instead. At 25 Delaware Avenue, the three-story courthouse (to be replaced a few years later with a more modern-looking eight-story one) stood right across the street from the city court building at 42 Delaware (a law firm occupies that building today). To submit the paperwork Ball had dispatched arresting officer Thomas Hennessey, who brought along Richard Edgington and his mother Judith.

The matter was heard by Erie County Judge William J. Regan, who listened to statements by Judith Edgington and two other witnesses to her boy's kidnapping (they were greenskeeper Sam Costa, who'd run Chyrel and Ritchie out of Delaware Park, and Elizabeth Hylant, who worked at Hertel and Saranac and had seen Ritchie being led away). And while Justice Partyka of City Court had ruled that his courtroom lacked authority to charge a minor with a kidnapping, the Honorable Judge Regan had a slightly different interpretation of the law.

He'd had to get creative, though. A 1956 amendment to Section 2186 of New York State penal law stipulated that, while criminal charges in general cannot be filed against a person under sixteen years of age, an exception could be made under a narrow set of circumstances. A child between the ages of fifteen and sixteen, the provision states, may be prosecuted as an adult if their alleged offense, had it been committed by an adult, would carry a punishment of either death or life imprisonment. In New York State kidnapping does carry a penalty of twenty to life, and on those grounds Judge Regan signed the warrant for Chyrel's arrest, marking the first time the new law had been applied in Erie County.

With Chyrel already being held at Meyer Memorial Hospital, the warrant was lodged with the hospital as a detainer, basically a written order for her to continue being held there until such time as she is deemed fit for arrest. She could be arraigned in either City Court or County Court, DA Ball told the *Buffalo Evening News*, and all evidence would be submitted to a grand jury, which was scheduled to meet on July 31.

Right away, though, Ball asked police to obtain either a signed written confession or an audio recording of the same. So, once again, Commissioner Felicetta headed out to Meyer Memorial, arranging to meet Dr. Yochelson there. There Chyrel repeated her confession, this time in the presence of a reel-to-reel recording machine.

The local papers' up-to-the-minute coverage of this case – the *Eve-*

*ning News* was averaging a few stories per day, carrying as many as six or seven separate articles on days with major developments – was also bringing forth a host of speculation from not just the general public, but also from area experts anxious to weigh in. Already there was speculation in the legal community that Chyrel's "confession," given the circumstances under which she'd made it, likely would be found inadmissible.

Even Dr. Yochelson, who'd drawn that confession from her in the first place, was now expressing concern that his patient was facing "trial by public opinion." On the occasion of her arrest, he told the *Evening News*, he had "pleaded" with photographers not to take Chyrel's picture. He'd also been "aghast," he declared, to learn that the name of a juvenile, not yet formally charged with any crime, had been released not just in print, but also in radio and television broadcasts.

What's more, Yochelson said, he'd been "surprised and chagrined to find that some of the details revealed to [him] by Cheryl, details which [he] discussed with the police but not with the press, had yet found their way into the press." He acknowledged the immense pressure being put on police to show they were making progress, but countered that "this does not alter the fact that in the minds of the public Cheryl, a minor, had already been convicted of this crime before she was charged with it or confessed any involvement."

That article also mentioned that this would be Dr. Yochelson's final summer in Buffalo, as he had recently been tapped to head the criminal psychiatry research department at St. Elizabeths Hospital in Washington, D.C. St. Elizabeths was then regarded as the country's premier mental health facility, and the work he'd done with Chyrel provided the perfect launchpad into that position. Yochelson would go on to achieve recognition for co-authoring *The Criminal Personality*, a three-volume work he'd collaborated on with a PhD named Stanton E. Samenow. Yochelson would die unexpectedly in 1976 after suffering a heart attack at a St. Louis airport.

\* \* \* \* \* \*

ON the morning of Sunday, July 9, Chyrel was transported from Meyer Memorial Hospital to Buffalo Police headquarters downtown.

At 10:30 a.m. she was administered a polygraph, which Commissioner Felicetta later told the *Buffalo Evening News* both Chyrel and her mother had agreed to. Dr. Yochelson was there, as well as Felicetta, a policewoman and Detective Sergeant John Rapp, who operated the polygraph. It was completed by noon, and neither Felicetta nor Yochelson would comment on the results. Chyrel was immediately taken back to the hospital, the *Evening News* noted, "in Commissioner Felicetta's private auto."

Notably absent from that whole ordeal was Chyrel's legal counsel, the right to which she was constitutionally entitled to. Her lawyer, actually, was at that very moment out on a limb trying to prevent the polygraph from even happening in the first place. Having learned that his client was about to be hooked up to a lie detector, L. Robert Leisner boldly called on New York State Supreme Court Justice William B. Lawless, Jr. at his home, presenting his Honor with paperwork that would prohibit police from questioning Chyrel any further.

Justice Lawless signed the temporary injunction around 11 a.m. – at which point Chyrel was mid-polygraph – placing her under the "custody, care and protection" of the New York State Supreme Court.

He further compelled the director of Meyer Memorial to appear in court to state why that order should not be made permanent. Most importantly, though, it prohibited all members of law enforcement and the district attorney's office from visiting Chyrel or questioning her in any capacity. Moving forward only Chyrel's parents, Dr. Yochelson and attorney Leisner would be allowed in to see her at the hospital.

At 10:30 a.m. that Tuesday, July 11, all interested parties were summoned to the county courthouse, where a conference was held in the chambers of New York State Supreme Court Justice Matthew J. Jasen. Psychiatrists from Meyer Memorial were there, and they advised Judge Jasen of their collective opinion that Chyrel was in fact mentally ill and therefore not fit to stand trial. Their report, they said, would be "imminent," so the judge adjourned the matter to Thursday, July 13, for further consideration.

The case was revisited on that day, with Justice Jason set to rule on Leisner's request that the temporary injunction preventing the questioning of his client be made permanent. First, however, the judge wanted to set a few things straight. It was alarming to him that, despite the fact that the warrant was issued a full week earlier, Chyrel had yet to been arraigned on the charge of Richard Edgington's kidnapping. The was "no valid reason," he said, for this not to have been done immediately, and he further reprimanded authorities for questioning and polygraphing the accused without her attorney present. The prosecution argued that the language in the temporary injunction technically barred them from carrying out the arraignment, so Judge Jasen vacated that portion of the order and directed them to get it done right away.

Accordingly, Chyrel was brought from Meyer Memorial to the county courthouse that very morning. Wearing a pink-checkered

summer dress, white shoes and her hair up in a pony, she was ushered directly into a private office just outside of Erie County Judge
William Regan's second-floor courtroom. Her arraignment was
scheduled for 11:30 a.m., but a one-hour delay was granted so Leisner could meet with Chyrel ahead of time, if only to explain to her
the arraignment process and what that meant moving forward.

Also in the courtroom was another attorney, William B. Mahoney,
who had been assigned by the New York State Bar Association to appear as *amicus curiae*, or, "friend of the court." In light of the recent
concerns raised by the ACLU, the Bar Association had, in the interest of justice, dispatched Mahoney to assist with Chyrel's defense,
and Leisner gladly welcomed him as co-counsel. The press, on the
other hand, was granted only limited access, and according to the
*Evening News* court deputies were instructed to "keep photographers
out of camera range of the girl."

Once Judge Regan had taken the bench, the *Evening News* reported, Chyrel was brought into the courtroom, where she sat "wide-
eyed" and "with her arms folded, facing the bench, and casting in-
quiring glances around the courtroom." The judge began reading the
formal proceedings, and when the word "kidnapping" was spoken
aloud Chyrel grew visibly emotional and teary. She did manage to
keep it together, though, largely thanks to the calm and reassuring
demeaner of attorney Mahoney.

Lawyer Leisner, meanwhile, took a louder, more brash and abra-
sive approach to defending his client. Immediately he interjected,
proclaiming he wanted to "challenge and defy" the court's jurisdiction, asking that the case be transferred to Children's Court. He was
overruled, and after waiving a full reading of the charges against
Chyrel, he and Mahoney entered a formal plea of not guilty. Judge
Regan then remanded Chyrel to Meyer Memorial Hospital, further

ordering that a psychological exam be performed there. Both Leisner and Mahoney objected to the psych eval, with Mahoney in fact questioning Regan's authority to order it. They were summarily overruled.

The whole thing only took about ten minutes, but by the time it was over Chyrel was all shook up and nearly in tears again. By the end of the day she was back at Meyer Memorial, where she would spend the next two weeks being formally evaluated and awaiting further charges in the death of Andrew Ashley.

* * * * * *

REGARDING the kidnapping and the killing of Andrew Ashley, the grand jury convened on Monday, July 31. Such proceedings are generally conducted in secret and behind closed doors, and Chyrel's case was no exception.

Presenting the prosecution's case was First Assistant District Attorney George R. Blair, who called in a string of witnesses to present the DA's contention that Chyrel was responsible for the kidnap and murder of Andrew Ashley, as well as for the earlier nabbing of Richard Edgington. Police Commissioner Frank Felicetta was called in, emerging about twenty-five minutes later and telling the *Buffalo Evening News* that, while he couldn't reveal the specifics of his testimony, he had stated and explained to the grand jury his role in the investigation. It was presumed, that paper reported, that Felicetta "related that the girl made an oral admission to him that she had bound the Ashley boy."

Another witness called was John Rapp, the detective sergeant who'd operated the polygraph during Chyrel's questioning back on

# Proceedings

July 9. It was believed, the *Evening News* reported, that Rapp played for the grand jury the tape recording made of Chyrel's confession on that day.

Chyrel's own mother, Georgia Jolls, was also called in, and she emerged with a curious story for reporters on hand to cover the affair. She'd been shut down, she said, for trying to introduce new information, information she felt might shed light on her daughter's state of mind when she was out (allegedly) committing these crimes. "I answered all the questions asked of me as well as I could," she told the *Evening News*, "and I think some attention should be given to my side of the story."

After Chyrel was arrested, Georgia explained, she'd found amongst her daughter's possession a handful of pills – four small white pills, as well as five gelatin caps with powder inside. These, she said, were seized by police after a second search of her home, but there had been no mention of them since and Georgia was adamant that they might have played a role in her daughter's unraveling. She did not know the nature of the drugs in question, but she suspected some of them were tranquilizers. "There are all kinds of tranquilizers," she said, "and I know when you take some of them you don't know whether you are coming or going."

Police, Georgia maintained, had also taken a note found alongside the pills, which she did not get a chance to read but felt might shed light on who had been supplying her daughter with these pills. Actually, she had her suspicions. Chyrel had a "strong allegiance," Georgia said, to a young woman who had always seemed a bit suspicious. The "most prominent and distinguishing thing about her," Georgia told the *Evening News*, "is that she has pinpoint eyes," then widely regarded a telltale sign of the soulless dope fiend.

Had Chyrel Jolls been operating under the influence of narcotics throughout the summer of 1961? Had she in fact been in some type of altered state while kidnapping three kids and killing one of them? Had this girl been driven by drugs to the commit the absolutely unthinkable? Her mother seemed to think so, revealing also that narcotics bureau detectives had questioned Chyrel at her school back on March 22, a month before her first known kidnapping.

The answers to these questions, it seems, are forever lost to history. First Assistant DA Blair insisted to Georgia that those pills and those capsules bore no absolutely no relevance to the case, and the issue would never again be raised in court. When pressed for comment the following day, Assistant Detective Chief John McCarthy told the *Evening News* that, to his knowledge, no drugs were seized from or even discovered at the Jolls residence. McCarthy then flat-out stated that he disbelieved Georgia's story, essentially implying she'd made the entire thing up from whole cloth.

* * * * * *

THAT Wednesday, August 2, the grand jury handed up its indictments, officially charging Chyrel Jolls with two counts – one for the kidnapping and first-degree murder of Andrew Ashley, the second for the kidnapping of Richard Edgington.

These were delivered to New York State Supreme Court Justice Alfred M. Kramer, who then summoned both the prosecution and the defense down to the county courthouse. Right away attorney Mahoney moved to have the case transferred to Children's Court, and right away Justice Kramer denied that request. Chyrel's case would instead be heard right there in County Court, to be presided over by the Honorable Judge Jacob A. Latona.

Chyrel was brought into Judge Latona's courtroom a little after 2:15 p.m. She'd been transported from Meyer Memorial Hospital to the Erie County Holding Center, then located at 10 Delaware Avenue, directly across from the county courthouse, which she entered via the "Tunnel of Tears," an underground passageway that runs beneath Delaware for the easy transport of high-profile defendants. Constructed in 1880, the 225-foot-long tunnel was designed to bypass any angry mobs that might assemble at street-level, its stone walls and low ceilings having hosted a slew famous culprits ranging from Leon Czolgosz (the assassin of President William McKinley in 1901) to Earl Simmons (the rapper DMX, arrested in 2001 for possession of marijuana and driving without a license).

Once inside, Chyrel was escorted up an elevator to the second floor, where the *Buffalo Evening News* reported that, "as photographers began snapping pictures, she started to scream and became upset. She remained in the judge's chambers with a woman deputy sheriff for a few minutes before going into the courtroom."

Outfitted in a white dress and with her hair again done up in a pony tail, Chyrel was given the option of waiting in the judge's chambers, but she chose to remain and spectators were instead ordered out of the courtroom, with the exception of the local papers. Leisner and Mahoney were there, and Mahoney again argued for a change of venue, insisting that his fifteen-year-old client was more suitable to be tried in Children's Court. A plea of not guilty was entered on Chyrel's behalf, and the matter was adjourned for further consideration.

As for the district attorney himself, Carman Ball bragged afterwards to the *Evening News* that Chyrel was in fact a local record-breaker. Not only was she the youngest person ever to be tried in Erie County for first-degree murder, he said, but this also marked the first time the county had ever tried a teenager for kidnapping.

The next day, back in Judge Latona's courtroom, Leisner and Mahoney continued arguing for a change of venue, insisting that his Honor did in fact have the authority to transfer the case to Children's Court. ADA Blair did not contest that point, actually, but the judge ruled that the matter hinged entirely on the results of the psych exam ordered by Judge Regan three weeks earlier. Until that report became available, he said, no action would be taken on that score.

But then, the following Monday, August 7, Judge Latona called a conference in his chambers, inviting both the prosecution and the defense in to discuss that very issue. It all came down to that pending report, really, but those examinations had been ordered by a different judge and Judge Latona now wanted a completely fresh and unbiased medical opinion. Ultimately, he ruled, the matter of jurisdiction would not be decided until completion of yet another comprehensive psychological work-up, this time by a team of doctors completely unattached to the case.

This evaluation, the judge said, was to be conducted by two separate and independent psychiatrists, and these psychiatrists were to be selected by Dr. Duncan Whitehead, the superintendent of Buffalo State Hospital. It would likely take several weeks, and Chyrel was to remain in custody at Meyer Memorial until the examinations were completed.

By the week's end Dr. Whitehead had chosen and appointed the two doctors who would evaluate Chyrel's mental state. Dr. Leonard Lang was an assistant director at Buffalo State Hospital, and Dr. Samuel Feinstein was the director of the regrettably-named New State

School for Retarded Children, which housed a wing that dealt exclusively with children's psychiatry. Each of them said their examination would likely take about three weeks.

\* \* \* \* \* \*

IT took closer to five.

On September 12 Dr. Lang and Dr. Feinstein both submitted their reports to the court, and the two of them were in agreement: Chyrel Jolls was mentally incompetent and therefore unfit to be tried in a court of law. It was more appropriate, they thought, that Chyrel be confined to a state facility until such time as she's sufficiently "recovered" and able to stand trial.

Chyrel's lawyers, however, were still keen to get her case transferred to Children's Court, where her punishment likely would be far less severe. This new report would certainly muddy those waters, so at the next hearing Leisner and Mahoney obtained a court order appointing two *more* psychiatrists, this time to be selected by the defense. They chose to have their client examined by Dr. James Robinson and Dr. Harold Graser, and weeks went by as each doctor conducted his own evaluation.

And, when Dr. Robinson and Dr. Graser reported their findings, it turned out that they had reached separate conclusions. It was Dr. Robinson's opinion that Chyrel was far too mentally ill to face a jury of her peers, while Dr. Graser apparently found otherwise. Dr. Robinson gave his opinion on the matter at Chyrel's next hearing, stating the girl suffered not from mental illness but something he called "character disorder." Dr. Graser was not called to testify one way or the other.

Now there was nothing to do but wait. Those hearings had lasted into the winter, and the city would ring in a new year before Judge Latona issued his formal decision. On Friday, January 12, 1962, the final hearing was held, with the judge at last ready to rule on the issue of Chyrel's sanity. Chyrel, this time, was not present in the court-room.

Having reviewed the reports and the testimony of all four psychiatrists, Judge Latona read out loud his four-page written opinion. Regard Chyrel's mental condition, he wrote, "the court feels that the opinion of Dr. Lang and Dr. Feinstein outweighed by far the opinion given by Dr. Robinson." It was Judge Latona's opinion, then, that Chyrel Jolls was insane and therefore immune from prosecution.

In such cases the law provides that the accused be committed to a psychiatric facility within the New York State Department of Corrections. Only one such facility existed, and it was located all the way downstate in the city of Beacon, about seventy miles north of New York City. That place would house Chyrel indeterminately and hopefully restore her to sanity, and Judge Latona signed the formal order to transfer her there.

Matteawan State Hospital for the Criminally Insane, essentially a holding pen for insane criminals, was enormous and beautiful, its campus made up of a cluster of regal-looking Victorian-style buildings. High fences and razor wire bordered the entire property, and those things would ensure that Chyrel remained confined there until she became of sound mind. No one could possibly say how long that would take, or if it would occur at all.

The following morning – Saturday, January 13, 1962 – Erie County Sheriff B. John Tutuska would escort Chyrel by train to Beacon, and then by taxi to Matteawan. With Chyrel Jolls now safely locked away – until further notice at least – the entire city of Buffalo breathed a tremendous sigh of relief.

# ELEVEN

# In The Interests Of Justice

**T**wo years passed.

Then, in March of 1964, Judge Jacob Latona received a letter from Dr. W.C. Johnston, superintendent of Matteawan State Hospital for the Criminally Insane. It concerned one of his patients, Chyrel Jolls, and he was writing to inform his Honor that the girl was "now mentally capable of standing trial."

Accordingly, Judge Latona signed an order directing the county sheriff to retrieve Chyrel, now eighteen years of age, and to transport her from Matteawan back to Buffalo for holding while prosecutors there geared up to bring her case to court. The transfer was made on Wednesday, April 1, and the defendant was remanded to the Erie County Holding Center downtown.

Chyrel was arraigned six weeks later, on May 13, in Erie County Court. As the indictments were read aloud she stood with her attorney, L. Robert Leisner, who chose not to enter a plea on his client's behalf. Still, its records indicate, the court entered a plea of not guilty and returned the defendant to jail, where she would spend the next five months awaiting trial.

On May 25 yet another psychiatric exam was ordered, and on June 19 the prosecution moved to bar Leisner from being present while it was conducted. This motion was upheld on July 31, and Chyrel's next court appearance was a brief one on August 31. The following month, on September 11, the two indictments – one for the first degree murder of Andrew Ashley and the other for the kidnapping of Richard Edgington – were consolidated for the sake of simplicity and of streamlining the proceedings.

The trial began on Monday, October 19, and it was presided over by the Honorable Charles J. Gaughan, a county justice appointed the previous year. The Erie County District Attorney, by this point, was Michael F. Dillon, whose office had scrambled to familiarize itself with all the details of this twisted case it had inherited from the previous administration. Jury selection had taken about two weeks, and attorney Leisner would later tell the *Buffalo Evening News* that Chyrel "had, in fact, assisted him during the selection of the 12-man jury."

At the trial's onset, Justice Gaughan later remarked to the *Evening News*, the defendant "seemed to be in normal mental health," but "her condition began to deteriorate soon after." Over the next five days of testimony, that paper reported, the courtroom watched as Chyrel's behavior went straight downhill. She smiled flirtatiously at one witness, and was overheard cursing at another. She drew up a note asking spectators to leave the courtroom. At one point, as

Georgia was giving her testimony, Chyrel removed one of her shoes, apparently intent on pelting her own mother with it right up there on the stand. During a tantrum she flushed her medicine down the toilet, and the *Evening News* also noted that "on several occasions, as witnesses testified that the girl they saw with the Edgington boy wore a pony tail," Chyrel "tried to simulate a pony tail by closing her hands around her hair."

Because of all this Judge Gaughan ordered yet another psychological examination, and he wanted it done immediately. As such, he requested that the two doctors charged with evaluating the defendant kindly do so at their earliest opportunity. They each agreed to meet with her that Sunday, November 15.

One of these doctors was Dr. Bruno Gustav Schutkeker, an area psychiatrist who was already known as a local pioneer in family and group therapy. He was known, too, for his sympathetic tendencies toward those charged with sometimes pretty awful offenses. From his obituary in the *Buffalo News*: "He testified frequently as an expert witness in court – always on behalf of the defense, the underdog, the criminally insane, colleagues said." The other, Dr. Armand L. DiFrancesco, was a supervising psychiatrist at nearby Buffalo State Hospital, and his obituary notes that he also was "a psychiatric consultant to the Erie County district attorney's office."

The following Tuesday, November 17, Judge Gaughan indicated to the courtroom that he had received and reviewed the psychiatrists' reports. Based on his reading of those, as well as his own observation of Chyrel's courtroom conduct, the judge flatly stated that it was his intention to declare a mistrial. He was doing so, he said, "out of a sheer sense of humaneness." The defendant's mental capacity, in his opinion, made prosecuting her for her crimes sadly inappropriate.

"The defendant has deteriorated both mentally and physically," he told the court. "It has become apparent that neither this defendant… nor the people can have a fair and impartial trial in this manner."

With a mistrial declared under those circumstances, and especially in light of Dr. Schutkeker's and Dr. DiFrancesco's reports, it was a near-certainty that Chyrel would be shipped back to Matteawan to remain incarcerated there indeterminately. This, to Leisner, was wholly unacceptable, as the maneuver would rob him of the opportunity to defend his client in open court. He would "not have any part" in sending her back to that facility, he declared, boldly telling the judge to his face that he intended to contest the psychiatric report and even the mistrial ruling itself.

Leisner wasn't through. He went on to interrupt the judge several times, quoting the U.S. Constitution and making a right spectacle of himself in general. Eventually Judge Gaughan held Leisner in contempt of court, cautioning him, "If you continue I will have you removed to the jail." With that the attorney settled down a bit, and the jury was brought in. Then, as the judge began addressing them, Leisner quite theatrically began packing up his briefcase. When asked what he was doing, the impudent lawyer shot back, "I see no reason for my staying here." Judge Gaughan saw otherwise, and he told the attorney to sit back down until he was told to leave.

At 10 a.m. the next day, November 18, a hearing was held to formally dissolve the court proceedings against Chyrel Jolls. Infuriated with the mistrial, Leisner pointed out that, as the two indictments against her would not be vacated, his client still faced the possibility of having to stand trial further down the road. "If the defendant is to be tried, now would be the time," he pleaded before the court. "While it might seem cruel it would be more humane than to bring her back for trial at a later date."

Leisner, still pretty heated about the psychiatric reports, then attempted to controvert them in the most outrageous manner imaginable. Stepping onto the witness stand, the lawyer called and then began questioning… himself. The *Evening News* reported on one especially amusing exchange: "At one point in his self-interrogation Mr. Leisner asked: 'Have you been assured of the confidence of the defendant?' His reply was: 'Will you please clarify the question more?'"

None of this worked. In the end a mistrial was officially declared, and Leisner wound up apologizing to the judge for his various outbursts. And, when Judge Gaughan advised that he would be requesting from DA Dillon an order sending Chyrel back to Matteawan, lawyer Leisner had but one meager request. It was a hardship on Georgia, he said, traveling more than three hundred miles each way to visit her daughter at that state-run facility. The remand to Matteawan would stand, although the judge did leave open the possibility of her later being moved to a more proximal facility, like Buffalo State Hospital.

Five days later, on Monday, November 23, Judge Gaughan signed the order confirming Chyrel's transfer, and for the final time she was escorted from the jail downtown to Matteawan downstate.

\* \* \* \* \* \*

ANOTHER five years went by.

By the winter of 1969 Chyrel had reached the age of twenty-three, and while it's tough to say exactly what day-to-day treatment at Matteawan consisted of, at least one doctor there was of the opinion that she had made considerable progress.

Dr. Leon Groth, a staff psychiatrist at the hospital, would later indicate that during this time Chyrel had, in many ways, "matured to a high degree." Emotionally, however, this was not the case, and he was fearful that the stress of another trial might trigger yet another breakdown. It was most appropriate, he thought, for the patient to be discharged from Matteawan, a state-run facility for the criminally insane, and committed instead to a civil hospital as the next step in her treatment and rehabilitation.

The courts, meanwhile, had appointed Chyrel a new attorney, a colorful and charismatic barrister named Robert M. Murphy. Murphy, according to a profile in the *Buffalo News* decades later, was known for combining his "street smarts with a photographic memory, a working-class background with a first-rate education, and a brawler's tenacity with a gentleman's manners, especially around juries and judges." Accordingly, he swiftly petitioned the court to hold a psychiatric hearing, and to release his client from Matteawan "in the interests of justice."

On Tuesday, November 18, Chyrel was brought from Matteawan to Buffalo, where deputies parked her back in the Erie County Holding Center. The next day a hearing was held at the county courthouse, where Murphy was advised by Joseph P. Burke, an administrative assistant in the district attorney's office, that DA Michael Dillon would first need to sign off on the formal dismissal of any charges. Burke was confident he could procure his boss's approval, and another hearing was set for November 25.

Chyrel appeared that day wearing a white sweater with a blue skirt, and by all accounts she remained calm and well-heeled. Her case, this time, was heard by Erie County Court Justice Frank R.

Bayger, who had been appointed to the bench the previous year. The court heard testimony from Dr. Groth of Matteawan, as well as from a local psychiatrist named Dr. Michael Lynch, both of whom were concurrent in their findings. Essentially, the *Buffalo Evening News* reported, the "two psychiatrists had testified that the woman was no longer psychotic, but warned she might revert to that state if she had to undergo any further trial proceedings."

"Before she can go into the community she needs pre-stage adjustment," Dr. Groth explained to the court. "Any further progression can only be afforded by a civil institution." An official okay from the district attorney had not yet been obtained, but administrative assistant Burke indicated he was expecting it by week's end. Another hearing was scheduled for that Friday, November 28.

Everything was in order on that date. Chyrel's transfer to a civilian-run hospital, rather than her continued confinement in a state-operated criminal institution, was agreed to by all parties concerned. One final court date was necessary, and it was docketed for December 17. The appearance would be a mere formality, and it would not be necessary for Chyrel to attend.

On Wednesday, December 17, the prosecution and the defense convened for the final time at the Erie County courthouse downtown. After reviewing a list of official "findings of facts," and also noting the district attorney's approval for the dismissal all charges, Judge Bayger summarily vacated the indictment against Chyrel Jolls. She would, he ruled, be remanded to a civil institution for further treatment, and that facility was to be selected by the commissioner of the New York State Department of Mental Hygiene.

It was certainly a victory for attorney Murphy, who praised the "courage" of both Judge Bayger and DA Michael Dillon, adding,

"This case convinces me that justice tempered with mercy exists in Erie County." In truth, everyone involved was no doubt glad to have this one off the books.

A reporter from the *Evening News* was there, and he or she took note of the defendant's conspicuous absence, as well as one other curious and lonely detail: "Miss Jolls, who was present at the hearing in November, was not present Wednesday. Her sister and a young child were the only spectators in the gallery."

\* \* \* \* \* \*

THE following month, in January 1970, it was decided that Chyrel would be sent to a facility almost three hundred miles away, all the way upstate and right on the Canadian border, closer to cities like Ottawa and Montreal than to Buffalo.

Ogdensburg is a small city on the St. Lawrence River, a one-time shipping hub thanks to its prime location along that busy trade route. Toward its eastern end, on nearly a thousand acres of rolling farmland, were the grounds of the St. Lawrence State Hospital, where Chyrel would be housed for further treatment and where she would remail until such time as considerable progress had been made. And, after five years locked away at Matteawan, she was no doubt pleasantly surprised, if not downright elated, with the comparatively-luxurious new accommodations.

Opened in 1890 as the Ogdensburg State Asylum for the Insane, the place was founded and even constructed with nothing but relaxation and serenity in mind. Its calm and sleepy campus was laid out in three groups of cottage-style buildings, and its founding superintendent, Dr. Peter M. Wise, had implemented what he called "moral treatment," which involved treating patients by first isolating them from every outside stressor imaginable.

Heavy emphasis, in fact, was placed on recreation and leisure, and on nurture and rest. There were countless activities, from music and dancing to movies and plays, with camping in the summer months and sledding and ice skating in the winter. The hospital even had its own steamboat, Dorothy, which took patients out for quick jaunts up and down the St. Lawrence River. At the same time, the hospital placed considerable focus on occupational therapy, meant to develop and help foster the discipline and mental focus required to operate in regular society. They even had, at that time, a functioning nursing school that trained patients deemed suitable for future employment in that field.

The hospital's most famous resident, by far, was Audrey Munson, arguably the first in a long line of young American starlets to spiral out of control and wind up institutionalized. A wildly popular artist's model during the Gilded Age – a slew of bronze sculptures and statues in New York City and elsewhere across the country bare her likeness – Munson had also starred in a few silent films, garnering the distinction of becoming, possibly, the first woman to appear completely nude in a non-pornographic film. By the 1920s her star had faded, though, and Munson had descended into the realm of bitterness, paranoia, antisemitism and all of that unpleasantness. There was a suicide attempt in 1922, and she had been committed to the St. Lawrence State Hospital since 1931, following an incident during which she'd assaulted a farmer with a pitchfork.

While being treated there for schizophrenia and depression, it is said, the one-time ingenue continued to put on all the animated airs of a major movie star, and the staff played right along. "They treated her like royalty there," her niece Darlene Bradley told Rochester's

*Democrat and Chronicle* in 2016, and as she aged Munson consistently resisted all efforts to have her transferred or discharged. Munson would, in fact, spend the rest of her life at that facility, remaining there until her death in 1996 at the age of 104. She would have been just seventy-eight in 1970, although there has been no evidence to suggest the unsung American icon ever met or interacted with the infamous Chyrel Jolls.

Then again, Chyrel was only there for about a year, all told. The hospital's records, according to the *Buffalo Courier-Express*, indicate that she was quietly and unceremoniously discharged on January 29, 1971, her medical files marked "released as cured."

Perhaps the treatment at the St. Lawrence State Hospital really was that good. Or, perhaps the place was low on beds and it needed the space. Certainly, the hospital would try decades later to expel old Audrey Munson as she neared the end of her own life, essentially for that second reason.

Either way, Chyrel had spent nearly a decade in confinement for her crimes – nine years, six months, three weeks and five days, to be precise – and while she had managed to avoid a full-on prison term, all that time spent as a ward of the state could only have left her permanently underdeveloped and, to some extent at least, forever institutionalized.

And now, having just turned twenty-five, she was free – entirely liberated from her past and legally immune to the possibility of any future prosecution. The hospital's records, the *Courier-Express* noted conclusively, "list Miss Jolls as having no address at the time of her release."

She was, in fact, for the remainder of her natural life, never to be heard from again.

Just like that, Chyrel Jolls was in the wind.

## TWELVE

# Do You Know Where Your Children Are?

"

**T**en years after her arrest in connection with the Ashley homicide, Chyrel Jolls has disappeared," the *Buffalo Courier-Express* wrote in July of 1971. By that time, the article noted, she would have been twenty-five years old, and already her whereabouts were completely unknown.

Her father Howard, for his part, hadn't been able to pull himself together and overcome his many demons, sadly. His alcoholism, in combination with a lifelong inability to support his wife and children, had apparently rendered him a broken, shellshocked husk of a man. The devastating scandal of Chyrel's heavily-publicized arrest and trial, presumably, had not helped, and by 1971 Howard was again institutionalized at the Gowanda State Hospital.

Georgia, on the other hand, had continued to soldier on. In the aftermath of Chyrel's arrest she had been forced to relocate, and according to Polk's Buffalo City Directory she resided at 136 North Pearl Street, apartment one, from 1963 until 1965. In 1967 an apartment at 120 North Pearl Street was listed as occupied by Nora Jolls, who was then twenty years old and presumably still living with her mother. By the following year, 1968, both Georgia and Nora had moved to 132 Elmwood Avenue, a two-story Allentown building that had once housed the New York Telephone Company.

Having gone on with her job at Buffalo General Hospital, Georgia retired in 1984 after twenty-five years as a food service worker in its cafeteria. She died there, actually, following an extended illness, at the age of seventy-nine on October 7, 1998. She is buried at Elmlawn Memorial Park, a cemetery in the nearby village of Kenmore. Her obituary, which appeared in the *Buffalo News*, gives no mention of Howard, although it does indicate that Georgia was survived by all seven of her children. One of them, the fourth one listed, is identified as "Cheryl of Watertown."

Chyrel Jolls, then, was alive as of 1998 and living in Watertown, another small city in Upstate New York, two hundred or so miles northeast of Buffalo and just below the Canadian border. Once a terrifically-wealthy shipping hub, the city underwent a large-scale deindustrialization process throughout the 1960s and 1970s, leading to a drastic decline in population and economic viability. Watertown is about sixty miles southwest of Ogdensburg, home of the St. Lawrence State Hospital, so perhaps Chyrel relocated there upon her 1971 discharge. What she was doing there, besides living in anonymity alongside a population with no knowledge of her disquieting past, is anyone's guess.

Chyrel's oldest brother, Alvin Jolls, passed away on February 4, 2010. His obituary, which ran in the *Buffalo News*, mentions that he had worked as a "painting contractor" and was survived by just three siblings – Henry, Estelle and Claire. Chyrel, by that logic, then, was deceased by the year 2010.

Her other brother, Henry Jolls, is still alive and believed to be living in the city of Buffalo.

Chyrel's older sister, Estelle, had gone on to marry a man named John Dovak, residing with him in Hastings, Ontario.

Clara, born right after Chyrel, went on to marry a man named Sparr and lives with him in Reading, Pennsylvania.

Barbara, the next Jolls kid sequentially, grew up to marry a man named Barca and they lived in Tulsa, Oklahoma. She was alive at the time of her mother's 1998 passing, but not her oldest brother's in 2010.

Finally, Chyrel's youngest and closest sibling Nora, who had lived with her mother all throughout Chyrel's tenure at Matteawan, eventually joined her sister Barbara in Tulsa, marrying a man named Weeden and raising a family with him there. Nora passed away on May 8, 2007 in Claremont, Oklahoma.

* * * * * *

ONCE Chyrel's case had been resolved, the people of Buffalo were finally able to exhale and move on. The citywide anxiety had quickly dissipated and all the excitement gradually died down, and the name Chyrel Jolls was swiftly forgotten, or at least reduced to hushed murmurs uttered in regretful tones.

Across the country, though, parents were rapidly waking up to the innumerable dangers that awaited their young, vulnerable and unsupervised children, particularly in dense, urban areas. This growing awareness was, in large part, thanks to the rising popularity of television broadcast news, and community leaders soon found themselves turning to that same medium to help combat this looming peril.

A senator in Massachusetts had, already by this point, proposed a nightly public service announcement, a nationwide reminder urging parents to be diligent with regards to their youngsters' late-night whereabouts. These were intended to air as introductory segments to each city's nightly news program, reminding viewers of the time (either ten or eleven o'clock, usually) and suggesting, not too subtly, that youngsters everywhere ought to be safely back at home or at the very least accounted for. The first high-profile use of such a PSA occurred in Los Angeles in 1964, and another began airing regularly in New York City a few years later.

These coordinated segments bore something of a catchphrase – "Do you know where your children are?" – and they were quick to become a cultural phenomenon, indelibly etched into the consciousness of just about every Baby Boomer and a huge swath of their kids. These adverts successfully caught on and gradually became standard countrywide, airing nightly from the mid-sixties and into the late-eighties.

That slogan, actually and quite appropriately, emerged out of Buffalo, New York, not too long after the whole Chyrel affair. Irv Weinstein, a local broadcaster, coined the phrase shortly after beginning his career at WKBW-TV, ABC's Buffalo affiliate, which aired locally on channel seven. Weinstein, who was known and beloved for his ability to turn a phrase, anchored that station's eleven o'clock "Eye-witness News" program from 1964 to 1998, and his line, less a legitimate question and more of a stark and confrontational warning, would go on to become wildly famous, often parodied and even gently lampooned on a 1996 episode of "The Simpsons."

"It's eleven o'clock. Do you know where your children are?"

According to WKBW's website, viewers tended to assume it was Weinstein's voice booming out that iconic line, drawing the night to a close with that stern and familiar catechism. It wasn't, though. The voiceover, curiously enough, was actually provided by the station's weatherman, who presented a nightly segment called "The Weather Outside" and would also become the widely-adored host of a long-running kids' program called "The Commander Tom Show."

That broadcaster's name, as a matter of fact, was Tom Jolls. His long and successful career at WKBW would span a full thirty-four years, culminating with his induction, alongside Weinstein and sports anchor Rick Azar, into the Buffalo Broadcasting Hall of Fame in 1998.

There is, in case you're wondering, no relation.

# Sources

**PROLOGUE**

1. Bernstein, Manuel, "Bound Body of Missing Boy Found in Delaware Park Lake," Buffalo Courier-Express, June 26, 1961.
2. "Child's Body Found In Isolated Part Of Delaware Lake," Buffalo Evening News, June 26, 1961.
3. "Unit Will Spearhead All-Out Search For Psychopathic Slayer," Buffalo Evening News, June 26, 1961.
4. "Obituaries" (Daniel F. Kennedy), Washington Post, April 5, 1988. Accessed online at https://www.washingtonpost.com/archive/local/1988/04/05/obituaries/f4b60dde-5009-4d8d-a79d-dded22319f52/

**ONE – Something Wicked This Way Comes**

1. "Woman Sought; Incident Second In Two Days," Buffalo Courier-Express, June 24, 1961.
2. Hale, Ed, "Last Man to See Boy Wishes He Had Been 'Nosy Neighbor,'" Buffalo Evening News, June 24, 1961.
3. "Kidnapper Viewed As Woman Who Lost Her Child," Buffalo Evening News, June 24, 1961.
4. "Neighbors Fearful After Third Victim Is Lured By Woman," Buffalo Evening News, June 24, 1961.
5. Batzer, Dick, "Find Killer Soon, Is Mother's Plea," Buffalo Courier-Express, June 26, 1961.
6. Bernstein, Manuel, "Bound Body of Missing Boy Found in Delaware Park Lake," Buffalo Courier-Express, June 26, 1961.

7. "Unit Will Spearhead All-Out Search For Psychopathic Slayer," Buffalo Evening News, June 26, 1961.

8. "Here's Sequence of Events In Murder of Ashley Boy," Buffalo Evening News, June 27, 1961.

9. Buell, Frank, "June 1961 – For the Ashleys, It Was to Be Month of Triumph," Buffalo Evening News, June 29, 1961.

10. "New, Detailed Description Of Andy's Killer Is Given," Buffalo Evening News, June 30, 1961.

11. Baldwin, Dick, "Uncle Believes Girl Innocent of Killing," Buffalo Courier-Express, July 6, 1961.

12. Spindler, Al, "Mrs. Jolls 'Very Sorry For Ashleys,'" Buffalo Courier-Express, July 6, 1961.

13. "Strands in Helmet Like Chyrel's Hair," Buffalo Courier-Express, July 6, 1961.

14. Continelli, Louise, "The Mind Of A Murderer: A Buffalo State Criminologist Tries To Fathom The Ultimate Act Of Violence," Buffalo News, May 20, 1990. Accessed online at https://buffalonews.com/news/the-mind-ofa-murderer-a-buffalo-state-criminologist-tries-to-fathom-the-ultimate-act-of/article_e6fb33d5-bdc4-597d-8aa1-d15682adae03.html

15. McLaughlin, Vance. The Postcard Killer. New York: Thunder's Mouth Press, 2006.

16. Rising, Gerry, "Scajaquada Creek," Buffalo News, September 23, 2007. Accessed online at http://www.acsu.buffalo.edu/~insrisg/nature/nw07/0923Scajaquada.htm

17. Glaeser, Edward L., "Can Buffalo Ever Come Back?" City Journal (website), Autumn 2007. Accessed online at https://www.city-journal.org/html/can-buffalo-ever-come-back-13050.html

18. Pelonero, Catherine, "Stranger with Candy: Why Did Teenager

Chyrel Jolls Kidnap, and Allegedly Murder, Children?" Catherine Pelonero (website), June 6, 2016. Accessed online at https://catherinepelonero.net/stranger-with-candy/

19. McNeil, Harold, "Delaware Park's Hoyt Lake fountain revived and running," Buffalo News, June 3, 2017. Accessed online at http://buffalonews.com/2017/06/02/hoyt-lake-fountain-delaware-park-turned-back/

20. Keppel, Angela, "The Many Lives of the Scajaquada: grassy banks, navy yard, battleground, trash dump, highway, creek," Discovering Buffalo, One Street At A Time (website), July 27, 2017. Accessed online at https://buffalostreets.com/2017/07/27/scajaquada/?fbclid=IwAR0n67mYuu-LPiENr8k2qLaexEJlGSm-bqIDY7OfyQ71Bu3BGay7uJe0OcI8

21. RaChaCha, "Olmstedian Scajaquada: The Scajaquada that Was and Wasn't," Buffalo Rising (website), December 11, 2019. Accessed online at https://www.buffalorising.com/2019/12/olmstedian-scajaquada-that-was-and-wasnt/

22. "Cheryl," babynames.net (website). Accessed online at https://babynames.net/names/cheryl

23. "Chyrel," names.org (website). Accessed online at https://www.names.org/n/chyrel/about

**TWO – An Ungovernable Minor**

1. Polk's Buffalo City Directory, 1961.
2. "Unit Will Spearhead All-Out Search For Psychopathic Slayer," Buffalo Evening News, June 26, 1961.
3. Wieland, Paul, "Girl Knew Andy Dead, Uncle Hints," Buffalo Courier-Express, July 5, 1961.

4. Burke, Dick, "Trail That Led to Cheryl Started When Patty Brown Told Mother," Buffalo Evening News, July 5, 1961.

5. Barnette, Ken, "'I Tried to Get Psychiatric Help for Cheryl,' Uncle Says," Buffalo Evening News, July 5, 1961.

6. Benevento, Mike, "Police Studying Cheryl's Diary," Buffalo Evening News, July 5, 1961.

7. "Can't Believe Cheryl Could Have Done This, Father Says," Buffalo Evening News, July 5, 1961.

8. "Police Quizzed Cheryl In Probe Of Fire At Home," Buffalo Evening News, July 5, 1961.

9. "Recheck of Suspects Led Detectives to Quiz Cheryl Again," Buffalo Evening News, July 5, 1961.

10. Baldwin, Dick, "Uncle Believes Girl Innocent of Killing," Buffalo Courier-Express, July 6, 1961.

11. Spindler, Al, "Mrs. Jolls 'Very Sorry For Ashleys,'" Buffalo Courier-Express, July 6, 1961.

12. "Strands in Helmet Like Chyrel's Hair," Buffalo Courier-Express, July 6, 1961.

13. "Ex Boy Friend Quotes Cheryl: 'I Hope They Get the Person,'" Buffalo Evening News, July 6, 1961.

14. "Partyka Says Court Lacks Jurisdiction On Warrant For Cheryl," Buffalo Evening News, July 6, 1961.

15. Continelli, Louise, "The Mind Of A Murderer: A Buffalo State Criminologist Tries To Fathom The Ultimate Act Of Violence," Buffalo News, May 20, 1990. Accessed online at https://buffalonews.com/news/the-mind-ofa-murderer-a-buffalo-state-criminologist-tries-to-fathom-the-ultimate-act-of/article_e6fb33d5-bdc4-597d-8aa1-d15682adae03.html

16. "Georgia Lois Jolls" (obituary), Buffalo News, October 9, 1998.

Accessed online at https://buffalonews.com/news/georgia-lo-is-jolls/article_5dd38018-7400-5370-bf66-366878f9ebd6. html?utm_medium=social&utm_source=email&utm_cam-paign=user-share

17. Hagmann, Douglas J., "Terror Targets U.S.: Islamic Jihad Training in America?" Canada Free Press (website), May 27, 2005. Accessed online at https://canadafreepress.com/2006/hag-mann052206.htm

18. McNamara, Pat, "The Good Shepherd Sisters, Buffalo, New York, 1914," McNamara's Blog (website), June 27, 2013. Accessed online at https://www.patheos.com/blogs/mcnama-rasblog/2013/06/the-good-shepherd-sisters-buffalo-new-york-1914.html

19. Sadowsky, Jonathan, "Electroconvulsive Therapy: A History of Controversy, but Also of Help," The Conversation (website), January 13, 2017. Accessed online at https://www.scientifi-camerican.com/article/electroconvulsive-therapy-a-histo-ry-of-controversy-but-also-of-help/

**THREE – Susie**

1. Polk's Buffalo City Directory, 1961.

2. "Area Where Boy Is Being Hunted," Buffalo Evening News, June 24, 1961.

3. "Boy Vanished Under Same Circumstances as 2 Others, Buffalo Evening News, June 24, 1961.

4. Benevento, Mike, "Bits Of Information Scrutinized In Effort To Get A 'Hard Clue,'" Buffalo Evening News, June 27, 1961.

5. Callahan, Bill, "Murder Probers To Intensify Check," Buffalo

Courier-Express, June 28, 1961.

6. "Fillmore-Leroy District Site of Hunt for Slayer," Buffalo Evening News, July 1, 1961.

7. Haines, Max, "Portrait of a kidnapper," Truro News (website), February 4, 2012. Accessed online at https://www.pressreader.com/canada/truro-news/20120204/282239482522514

## FOUR – Ritchie

1. Polk's Buffalo City Directory, 1961.

2. "Woman Sought; Incident Second In Two Days," Buffalo Courier-Express, June 24, 1961.

3. "Boy Vanished Under Same Circumstances as 2 Others, Buffalo Evening News, June 24, 1961.

4. Benevento, Mike, "Bits Of Information Scrutinized In Effort To Get A 'Hard Clue,'" Buffalo Evening News, June 27, 1961.

5. Callahan, Bill, "Murder Probers To Intensify Check," Buffalo Courier-Express, June 28, 1961.

6. Benevento, Mike, "Strands of Hair Analyzed In Hunt for Kidnap-Killer," Buffalo Evening News, June 30, 1961.

7. "New, Detailed Description Of Andy's Killer Is Given," Buffalo Evening News, June 30, 1961.

8. "New Tips Checked In Murder Enquiry," Buffalo Courier-Express, July 1, 1961.

9. "Fillmore-Leroy District Site of Hunt for Slayer," Buffalo Evening News, July 1, 1961.

10. Bernstein, Manuel, "Edgington Boy And Police Retrace Abductor's Route," Buffalo Courier-Express, July 3, 1961.

11. "5-Year-Old Boy Gives New Insight On Ashley Killer," Buffalo

Evening News, July 3, 1961.

12. "Partyka Says Court Lacks Jurisdiction On Warrant For Cheryl," Buffalo Evening News, July 6, 1961.

13. "Kidnap Warrant Issued After Statements by Boy's Mother, Others," Buffalo Evening News, July 7, 1961.

14. "Buffalo Zoo," Wikipedia (website). Accessed online at https://en.wikipedia.org/wiki/Buffalo_Zoo

15. Moran, Jay, "Monument honors Buffalo's War of 1812 veterans," WBFO (website), May 25, 2012. Accessed online at https://www.wbfo.org/local/2012-05-25/monument-honors-buffalos-war-of-1812-veterans?_amp=true&fbclid=I-wAR11iLw-C20ATunQ6vOj7naEUHODhkgqwSMEzo-2He-NNdSjZCwBDhwTzR8s

16. Cichon, Steve, "The Mound in the Meadow: Buffalo's Tomb of the Unknowns at Delaware Park," Buffalo Stories (website). Accessed online at http://blog.buffalostories.com/the-mound-in-the-meadow-buffalos-tomb-of-the-unknowns-at-delaware-park/

17. Pelonero, Catherine, "Stranger with Candy: Why Did Teenager Chyrel Jolls Kidnap, and Allegedly Murder, Children?" Catherine Pelonero (website), June 6, 2016. Accessed online at https://catherinepelonero.net/stranger-with-candy/

**FIVE – Andy**

1. Polk's Buffalo City Directory, 1961.

2. "Woman Sought; Incident Second In Two Days," Buffalo Courier-Express, June 24, 1961.

3. Hale, Ed, "Last Man to See Boy Wishes He Had Been 'Nosy

Neighbor,'" Buffalo Evening News, June 24, 1961.

4.  "Kidnapper Viewed As Woman Who Lost Her Child," Buffalo Evening News, June 24, 1961.

5.  "Neighbors Fearful After Third Victim Is Lured By Woman," Buffalo Evening News, June 24, 1961.

6.  Batzer, Dick, "Find Killer Soon, Is Mother's Plea," Buffalo Courier-Express, June 26, 1961.

7.  Bernstein, Manuel, "Bound Body of Missing Boy Found in Delaware Park Lake," Buffalo Courier-Express, June 26, 1961.

8.  "Unit Will Spearhead All-Out Search For Psychopathic Slayer," Buffalo Evening News, June 26, 1961.

9.  "Here's Sequence of Events In Murder of Ashley Boy," Buffalo Evening News, June 27, 1961.

10. Benevento, Mike, "Hunt For Murderer Of Young Ashley Boy Extends To Erie, PA.," Buffalo Evening News, June 28, 1961.

11. Buell, Frank, "June 1961 – For the Ashleys, It Was to Be Month of Triumph," Buffalo Evening News, June 29, 1961.

12. "Cheryl Questioned, Released Four Times During Week," Buffalo Evening News, July 5, 1961.

13. "Recheck of Suspects Led Detectives to Quiz Cheryl Again," Buffalo Evening News, July 5, 1961.

**SIX – Patty and Elizabeth**

1.  Polk's Buffalo City Directory, 1961.

2.  Buell, Frank, "Andy's Parents Can't Believe It – 'It's Something You Read About,'" Buffalo Evening News, June 24, 1961.

3.  "Neighbors Fearful After Third Victim Is Lured By Woman," Buffalo Evening News, June 24, 1961.

4. Bernstein, Manuel, "Bound Body of Missing Boy Found in Delaware Park Lake," Buffalo Courier-Express, June 26, 1961.

5. "Here's Sequence of Events In Murder of Ashley Boy," Buffalo Evening News, June 27, 1961.

6. Spindler, Al, "Ashley Murder Suspect Quizzed, Set Free Earlier," Buffalo Courier-Express, July 4, 1961.

7. Wieland, Paul, "Girl Knew Andy Dead, Uncle Hints," Buffalo Courier-Express, July 5, 1961.

8. Burke, Dick, "Trail That Led to Cheryl Started When Patty Brown Told Mother," Buffalo Evening News, July 5, 1961.

9. "Cheryl Questioned, Released Four Times During Week," Buffalo Evening News, July 5, 1961.

## SEVEN – "We Are Dealing With A Woman Maniac"

1. Batzer, Dick, "Find Killer Soon, Is Mother's Plea," Buffalo Courier-Express, June 26, 1961.

2. Bernstein, Manuel, "Bound Body of Missing Boy Found in Delaware Park Lake," Buffalo Courier-Express, June 26, 1961.

3. "Child's Body Found In Isolated Part Of Delaware Lake," Buffalo Evening News, June 26, 1961.

4. "Unit Will Spearhead All-Out Search For Psychopathic Slayer," Buffalo Evening News, June 26, 1961.

5. Benevento, Mike, "Bits Of Information Scrutinized In Effort To Get A 'Hard Clue,'" Buffalo Evening News, June 27, 1961.

6. "Buffalo's Postmen Helping Hunt for Andy's Murderer," Buffalo Evening News, June 27, 1961.

7. Callahan, Bill, "Murder Probers To Intensify Check," Buffalo Courier-Express, June 28, 1961.

8.  Benevento, Mike, "Hunt For Murderer Of Young Ashley Boy Extends To Erie, PA.," Buffalo Evening News, June 28, 1961.

9.  "Torn Toweling Found At Park Lake Matches Fabric On Boy's Body," Buffalo Evening News, June 29, 1961.

10. "Lake Yields Boy's Trousers," Buffalo Courier-Express, June 30, 1961.

11. Benevento, Mike, "Strands of Hair Analyzed In Hunt for Kidnap-Killer," Buffalo Evening News, June 30, 1961.

12. "New, Detailed Description Of Andy's Killer Is Given," Buffalo Evening News, June 30, 1961.

13. "Fillmore-Leroy District Site of Hunt for Slayer," Buffalo Evening News, July 1, 1961.

14. Bernstein, Manuel, "Edgington Boy And Police Retrace Abductor's Route," Buffalo Courier-Express, July 3, 1961.

15. O'Neill, Marty and LaHoud, John, "Girl, 15, Named; Meyer Hospital Tests Are Next," Buffalo Courier-Express," July 4, 1961.

16. Wieland, Paul, "Girl Knew Andy Dead, Uncle Hints," Buffalo Courier-Express, July 5, 1961.

17. "Man Says He Told Police About Girl," Buffalo Courier-Express, July 5, 1961.

18. West, Jack, "Hair In Toy Helmet Is Key To Possible Case Against Cheryl," Buffalo Evening News, July 5, 1961.

19. "Cheryl Questioned, Released Four Times During Week," Buffalo Evening News, July 5, 1961.

20. "FBI Says Hair in Helmet Has Cheryl's Characteristics," Buffalo Evening News, July 6, 1961.

21. "Samuel Yochelson," jbuff.com (website). Accessed online at http://jbuff.com/syoc.htm

## EIGHT – Another Look

1. Franken, Rose. Claudia and David. Philadelphia: Triangle Books, 1946.
2. Polk's Buffalo City Directory, 1961.
3. "5-Year-Old Boy Gives New Insight On Ashley Killer," Buffalo Evening News, July 3, 1961.
4. O'Neill, Marty and LaHoud, John, "Girl, 15, Named; Meyer Hospital Tests Are Next," Buffalo Courier-Express," July 4, 1961.
5. Wieland, Paul, "Girl Knew Andy Dead, Uncle Hints," Buffalo Courier-Express, July 5, 1961.
6. Barnette, Ken, "'I Tried to Get Psychiatric Help for Cheryl,' Uncle Says," Buffalo Evening News, July 5, 1961.
7. Benevento, Mike, "Police Studying Cheryl's Diary," Buffalo Evening News, July 5, 1961.
8. West, Jack, "Hair In Toy Helmet Is Key To Possible Case Against Cheryl," Buffalo Evening News, July 5, 1961.
9. "Cheryl Questioned, Released Four Times During Week," Buffalo Evening News, July 5, 1961.
10. "Recheck of Suspects Led Detectives to Quiz Cheryl Again," Buffalo Evening News, July 5, 1961.
11. "Strands in Helmet Like Chyrel's Hair," Buffalo Courier-Express, July 6, 1961.
12. "Ex Boy Friend Quotes Cheryl: 'I Hope They Get the Person,'" Buffalo Evening News, July 6, 1961.
13. "FBI Says Hair in Helmet Has Cheryl's Characteristics," Buffalo Evening News, July 6, 1961.

## NINE: A Reluctant Confession

1. West, Jack, "Hair In Toy Helmet Is Key To Possible Case Against Cheryl," Buffalo Evening News, July 5, 1961.
2. "Can't Believe Cheryl Could Have Done This, Father Says," Buffalo Evening News, July 5, 1961.
3. Spindler, Al, "Mrs. Jolls 'Very Sorry For Ashleys,'" Buffalo Courier-Express, July 6, 1961.
4. "Strands in Helmet Like Chyrel's Hair," Buffalo Courier-Express, July 6, 1961.
5. "ACLU Expresses Its Concern Over Handling of Cheryl," Buffalo Evening News, July 6, 1961.
6. "FBI Says Hair in Helmet Has Cheryl's Characteristics," Buffalo Evening News, July 6, 1961.
7. "Partyka Says Court Lacks Jurisdiction On Warrant For Cheryl," Buffalo Evening News, July 6, 1961.
8. Popiel, Al, "Grand Jury Will Consider Murder, Kidnaping Cases," Buffalo Evening News, July 7, 1961.
9. "Delicate Legal Problems Arise in Cheryl's 'Confession,'" Buffalo Evening News, July 7, 1961.
10. "Detectives Hailed By Erie Club Chief In Ashley Case," Buffalo Evening News, July 7, 1961.
11. "Kidnap Warrant Issued After Statements by Boy's Mother, Others," Buffalo Evening News, July 7, 1961.
12. West, Jack, "Lawyer Obtains Court Order Putting Cheryl in Seclusion," Buffalo Evening News, July 10, 1961.
13. "Was Denied Access To Cheryl, Family Attorney Charges," Buffalo Evening News, July 11, 1961.
14. "Carmen Ball, 97, justice in prison riot trials; Feb. 11, 1915

– March 26, 2012," Buffalo News, March 29, 2012. Accessed online at https://buffalonews.com/news/carman-ball-97-justice-in-attica-prison-riot-trials-feb-11-1915---/article_6eb35e4c-5068-5b1c-b245-9d984f431aa9.html

15. "A Brief History of the Erie County Medical Center," ECMC (website). Accessed online at https://www.ecmc.edu/about-ec-mc/a-brief-history-of-the-erie-county-medical-center/

## TEN – Proceedings

1. Colligan, Frank, "Charged Against Cheryl Based On a Rarely-Used Clause," Buffalo Evening News, July 7, 1961.

2. "Delicate Legal Problems Arise in Cheryl's 'Confession,'" Buffalo Evening News, July 7, 1961.

3. "Doctor Protests 'Trial by Opinion' Of Cheryl Jolls," Buffalo Evening News, July 7, 1961.

4. "Kidnap Warrant Issued After Statements by Boy's Mother, Others," Buffalo Evening News, July 7, 1961.

5. "Police Examine Cheryl's Story of Leaving Boy Alive," Buffalo Evening News, July 8, 1961.

6. West, Jack, "Lawyer Obtains Court Order Putting Cheryl in Seclusion," Buffalo Evening News, July 10, 1961.

7. Colligan, Frank, "Psychiatrists Ready To Inform The Court: Cheryl Mentally Ill," Buffalo Evening News, July 11, 1961.

8. Colligan, Frank, "Authorities Weigh Their Next Steps In the Jolls Case," Buffalo Evening News, July 12, 1961.

9. Colligan, Frank, "Cheryl Is Arraigned And Pleads Innocent To Kidnaping Charge," Buffalo Evening News, July 13, 1961.

10. "Injunction Is Vacated By Jasen," Buffalo Evening News, July 13, 1961.

11. "Mother Calls for an Inquiry About Capsules Cheryl Had," Buffalo Evening News, August 1, 1961.

12. Colligan, Frank, "Indictments Charge Girl With Murder, Kidnaping," Buffalo Evening News, August 2, 1961.

13. "Police Deny They Found Capsules In Cheryl's Room," Buffalo Evening News, August 2, 1961.

14. "Law Gives Latona Authority To Transfer Cheryl's Case," Buffalo Evening News, August 3, 1961.

15. Colligan, Frank, "New Mental Test for Cheryl Ordered by Judge Latona," Buffalo Evening News, August 7, 1961.

16. Colligan, Frank, "Ball Reports He's Doubtful Cheryl Could Stand Trial," Buffalo Evening News, August 8, 1961.

17. "Chyrel's Ability to Stand Trial Is Doubted by DA," Buffalo Courier-Express, August 9, 1961.

18. "Two Named To Examine Chyrel Jolls," Buffalo Courier-Express, August 11, 1961.

19. Colligan, Frank, "Cheryl Jolls Believed Found To Be Mentally Incompetent," Buffalo Evening News, September 12, 1961.

20. Colligan, Frank, "Cheryl Jolls Going To State Hospital; Trial Is Ruled Out," Buffalo Evening News, January 12, 1962.

21. "Chyrel to Be Committed," Buffalo Courier-Express, January 13, 1962.

22. Michel, Lou, "'Tunnel of Tears' To Move Inmates Is A Still-Functional Piece Of History," Buffalo News, October 13, 2001. Accessed online at https://buffalonews.com/news/tunnel-of-tears-to-move-inmates-is-a-still-functional-piece-of-history/article_f70c09a9-a4d7-57fc-8122-2e09740047ee.html

23. Gallivan, Peter, "The Tunnel of Tears, A Subterranean Link to Buffalo History," WGRZ (website), September 11, 2018.

Accessed online at https://www.wgrz.com/article/news/
the-tunnel-of-tears-a-subterranean-link-to-buffalo-histo-
ry/71-592942422

24. Lendzian, Daniel, "Haunted History: Old County Hall is at
the center of Buffalo's most dramatic moments," Buffalo Rising
(website), October 28, 2020. Accessed online at https://www.
buffalorising.com/2020/10/haunted-history-old-county-hall/

25. "Matteawan State Hospital for the Criminally Insane," Wikipedia (website). Accessed online at https://en.wikipedia.org/wiki/
Matteawan_State_Hospital_for_the_Criminally_Insane

## ELEVEN – In The Interests Of Justice

1. "Chyrel Jolls Ruled Able to Stand Trial," Buffalo Courier-Express, March 24, 1964.

2. Colligan, Frank, "Cheryl Jolls Awaiting Trial 3 Years After Infant's Death," Buffalo Evening News, June 23, 1964.

3. "Cheryl Jolls Case In Boy's Kidnaping Declared Mistrial," Buffalo Evening News, November 17, 1964.

4. "Defense Lawyer to Fight Jolls Case Mistrial Rule," Buffalo Courier-Express, November 18, 1964.

5. "Judge Orders Cheryl Jolls Committed to State Hospital," Buffalo Evening News, November 19, 1964.

6. "The People Of The State Of New York Against Chyrel Jolls,"
Erie County Court criminal records department, 1964 and
1969.

7. "Cheryl Jolls Awaits Hearing in 1961 Child Slaying," Buffalo
Evening News, November 20, 1969.

8. "Judge Adjourns Jolls Hearing," Buffalo Courier-Express, November 26, 1969.

9. "Charges Dismissed In Jolls Case," Buffalo Evening News, December 18, 1969.

10. Schwerzler, Nancy, "Update: Chyrel Jolls," Buffalo Courier-Express, July 23, 1971.

11. "Dr. Armand L. DiFrencesco, 67, Dies; Was Psychiatrist, Researcher," Buffalo News, November 18, 1988. Accessed online at https://buffalonews.com/news/dr-armand-l-difrancesco-67-dies-was-psychiatrist-researcher/article_027b2bfe-e312-5bbb-b2ba-b24fa27b318d.html?utm_medium=social&utm_source=email&utm_campaign=user-share

12. Cardinale, Anthony, "Dr. Bruno Schutkeker Dies; Psychiatrist Pioneered Family, Group Therapy Here," Buffalo News, January 1, 1991. Accessed online at https://buffalonews.com/news/dr-bruno-schutkeker-dies-psychiatrist-pioneered-family-group-therapy-here/article_f08e0b6e-b7ed-574d-89a2-525cde37321b.html?utm_medium=social&utm_source=email&utm_campaign=user-share

13. "Tribute for Robert Murphy '56 raises funds for mock trial teams," UB Law Forum, October 1, 2001.

14. Spevak, Jeff, "America's first nude supermodel was born in Rochester," Democrat and Chronicle, April 29, 2016. Accessed online at https://www.democratandchronicle.com/story/lifestyle/2016/04/29/americas-first-nude-supermodel-born-rochester/83656636/

15. "Saint Lawrence State Hospital," Opacity (website). Accessed online at https://opacity.us/site53_saint_lawrence_state_hospital.htm

16. "St. Lawrence State Hospital," Asylum Projects (website). Ac-

cessed online at https://www.asylumprojects.org/index.php/
St._Lawrence_State_Hospital

**TWELVE – Do You Know Where Your Children Are?**

1. Polk's Buffalo City Directory, 1962, 1963, 1964, 1965, 1966, 1967, 1968 and 1969-1970

2. Schwerzler, Nancy, "Update: Chyrel Jolls," Buffalo Courier-Express, July 23, 1971.

3. "Georgia Lois Jolls" (obituary), Buffalo News, October 9, 1998. Accessed online at https://buffalonews.com/news/georgia-lois-jolls/article_5dd38018-7400-5370-bf66-366878f9ebd6. html?utm_medium=social&utm_source=email&utm_campaign=user-share

4. "Nora Weeden" (obituary), Tulsa World (website), May 10, 2007. Accessed online at https://www.legacy.com/us/obituaries/tulsaworld/name/nora-weeden-obituary?id=27988036

5. "Jolls, Alvin H. 'Painting Contractor'" (obituary), Buffalo News, February 7, 2010. Accessed online at https://buffalonews.com/obituaries/jolls-alvin-h-painting-contractor/article_f29f1dc3-c82a-55fe-9610-ee715fb308db.html

6. "Celebrating WKBW's history: 60 years serving WNY," WKBW (website), November 18, 2018. Accessed online at https://www.wkbw.com/about-us/60th-anniversary/celebrating-wkbws-history-60-years-serving-wny

7. "Do you know where your children are?" The Weather Channel Wiki (website). Accessed online at https://weatherchannel.fandom.com/wiki/Do_you_know_where_your_children_are%3F

8. "Irv Weinstein," Wikipedia (website). Accessed online at https://

en.wikipedia.org/wiki/Irv_Weinstein

9. "Tom Jolls," Wikipedia (website). Accessed online at https://en.wikipedia.org/wiki/Tom_Jolls

10. Elmlawn Memorial Park, burial records.

www.ingramcontent.com/pod-product-compliance
Lightning Source LLC
Chambersburg PA
CBHW060908280326
41934CB00007B/1231